O

CANADIAN QUOTES

Lisa Wojna

First printed in 2005 10 9 8 7 6 5 4 3 2
Printed in Canada

The Publisher: Blue Bike Books Ltd.

Library and Archives Canada Cataloguing in Publication

Wojna, Lisa, 1962–
Bathroom book of Canadian quotes / Lisa Wojna.

(Bathroom books of Canada ; 4)
ISBN-13: 978-1-897278-01-7
ISBN-10: 1-897278-01-2

1. Quotations, Canadian (English). 2. Canada—Quotations, maxims, etc.
I. Title. II. Series.

PN6084.C15W64 2006 C818'.02 C2006-900619-9

Project Director: Nicholle Carrière
Project Editor: Tom Monto
Illustrations: Roger Garcia
Cover Image: Roger Garcia

PC:P5

DEDICATION

To my eldest, Peter—always deep in thought.

ACKNOWLEDGEMENTS

Writing may be a solitary occupation, but the journey of putting a book together is far from a solitary one. Completing this book on Canadian quotes would not have been possible without the keen eyes and quick mind of editor Tom Monto. Thank you for catching my errors and preventing me from a forced inclusion into this book's blooper section. Thank you to my publisher—you've seen me through a tough year and didn't give up on me when countless others would have. As always, thank you to my children, Peter, Melissa, Matthew and Nathaniel—you are all a constant source of inspiration. And finally, thank you to my husband, Garry, and to our beautiful granddaughter, Jada.

CONTENTS

WELCOME TO OUR WORLD

EARNING YOUR KEEP

LIFE AND THE ART OF LIVING

BREAKING NEW GROUND

TORIES, GRITS AND ASSORTED EXTRAS

SOMETHING TO THINK ABOUT

WE GOT GAME

INTRODUCTION

"Don't count your chickens before they hatch."

When I was a youngster, my mother repeated this old adage so many times I learned it well and quickly paired it with a maxim spoken by an older sister, "Don't count on anything; that way you're never disappointed." My sister, 12 years my senior, reached the "jaded stage" of life long before I did. Although I love them both dearly, I found their collective outlook rather limiting. How about hope and faith and laughter and love? Weren't there any sayings about them?

I looked and listened and quickly discovered there's a quote for just about every life circumstance. Some quotes—the happier, challenging, uplifting ones—became a lifeline of sorts for me while I was going through the tumultuous teen years. Even today, the walls of my office are plastered with such sayings, just in case I need an extra boost for one reason or other. Whenever I'm feeling down, I look up and read Rudyard Kipling's famous lines: "If you can keep your head when all about you are losing theirs..." When I'm feeling an attack of self-pity, I look up and read this quote from Canadian writer Thomas H. Raddall: "Never run from anything till you've had a good look at it. Most times it's not worth running from." When I'm frustrated, I look up at my inspirational calendar with a quote for every month. It's the only calendar I've ever broken down to purchasing as I usually just use the freebie giveaways from local banks and retail outlets.

So when I thought to do a book on Canadian quotations, it seemed a natural fit—and a fairly simple assignment. Collect wise comments from recognizable Canadians and *voila*—project complete.

I, the quotation queen with proverbs for just about any situation you can imagine memorized and ready for recitation at the appropriate moment, should have known better. But we're all a little narrow-minded and I, being a sappy sort of person, gravitate to a certain kind of quote. You know, those make-life-better kinds. Those challenge-yourself-to-greater-heights kind. Those every-dark-cloud-has-a-silver-lining kind.

As I perused the words of many a great Canadian something-or-other, I quickly realized Canadian quotations fall into a far larger assortment of themes than I usually collect. Some of them were quite horrendous, stripping me of my notions that my beloved country's history doesn't have situations so damning they could be put into a category labeled "hateful." Some, on the other hand, were funny—really very funny. So it was back to the drawing board, so to speak, to redefine for myself what a quote really was.

A quote: a collection of words strung together. When uttered by someone of notoriety or public status, these words are often promoted from the realm of casual comment to that of an utterance worth bearing repetition and for some, a home in the treasure trove of commonly repeated sayings—otherwise known as maxims, adages, mottos, aphorisms, saws, proverbs and bywords.

Of course, some quotes are quite the opposite. Instead of graduating to the status of wise aphorisms, they are conferred with the less honourable title of blunders—otherwise known as bloopers, slip-ups, booboos, indiscretions, *faux pas*, dumb moves, and just plain "Oh my gosh I can't believe I just said that" gaffes.

While researching this collection, I've gained an appreciation of how much Canadians value their natural resources, how our artists and writers are as challenging and profound as their predecessors in antiquity and how our pioneering women fought for and achieved a solid foundation for recognition and equality. I also learned that politics can be extremely funny. I had to reserve an entire section under the "blunder, blooper and booboo" category for comments from the people who run this country.

While reading thousands upon thousands of quotes, I learned which of my literary heroes were a tad jaded and which were truly patriotic. I learned how my tendency to self-criticize is a universal Canadian trait—Canadians criticize just about everything they can about Canada from something as trivial as the weather to whether we're living up to our reputation as world peacekeepers. I also discovered at least one person of note whose positive attitude never failed to amaze me—and he's a politician at that! Good ol' former prime minister Joe Clark, quoted hundreds of times in dozens of sources, easily earns the title of Canadian cheerleader par excellence, uttering nary a quote with anything less than a rah-rah for the great country we live in.

Always insightful, often wise, frequently funny, habitually challenging and occasionally macabre, the quotes in this collection give us a glimpse of what it is to be Canadian—our history, our unique world perspectives and even our tendency toward self-deprecation.

Agree or disagree with the sentiment behind these quotes. Laugh at some. Take comfort in still others. No matter what your thoughts, one thing is certain: these Canadian quotes will leave you with something to think about.

PURELY CANADIAN, EH?

You know you're Canadian when you apologize to the guy behind you in the supermarket checkout after he slams his shopping cart into your backside. You know you're Canadian when you find a five-dollar bill on the ground and turn it in at your local police station. A Canadian knows that a loonie is not just a bird or a nutcase, but also a dollar coin. And that when you ask for a mickey, you're talking about something far different than the friendly Disney mouse.

A CANADIAN IS...

Let's see what Canadians have to say for themselves.

I am Canadian, free to speak without fear, free to worship in my own way, free to stand for what I think right, free to oppose what I believe wrong, or free to choose those who shall govern my country. This heritage of freedom I pledge to uphold for myself and all mankind.

–From the Canadian Bill of Rights, July 1, 1960

I just am a Canadian. It is not a thing which you can escape from. It is like having blue eyes.

–Robertson Davies (1913–95), writer

Under this flag may our youth find new inspiration for loyalty to Canada; for a patriotism based not on any mean or narrow nationalism, but on the deep and equal pride that all Canadians will feel for every part of this good land.

–Lester B. Pearson (1897–1972), prime minister

It is wonderful to feel the grandness of Canada in the raw, not because she is Canada but because she's something sublime that you were born into, some great rugged power that you are a part of.

–Emily Carr (1871–1945), artist and writer

Canadians are the people who learned to live without the bold accents of the natural ego-trippers of other lands.

–Marshall McLuhan (1911–80), educator and media philosopher

Our hopes are high. Our faith in the people is great. Our courage is strong. And our dreams for this beautiful country will never die.

–Pierre Elliott Trudeau (1919–2000), prime minister

We have it all. We have great diversity of people, we have a wonderful land, and we have great possibilities. So all those things combined there's nowhere else I'd rather be.

–Bob Rae (1948–), Ontario premier

Canadians are a meek bunch; they'll take orders from anybody in uniform, including the milkman.

–Arthur Reginald Marsden (A.R.M.) Lower (1889–1988), historian and sailor, in 1951

We shall be Canadians first, foremost, and always, and our policies will be decided in Canada and not dictated by any other country.

–John G. Diefenbaker (1895–1979), prime minister

What we do should have a Canadian character. Nobody looks his best in somebody else's clothes.

–Vincent Massey (1887–1967), governor general of Canada

A Canadian is someone who knows how to make love in a canoe.

–Pierre Berton (1920–2004), writer

Vive la Canada. This country is not for sale.

–Don Sweet, Canadian football player

If you don't believe your country should come before yourself,
you can better serve your country by livin' someplace else.

–"Stompin' Tom" Connors (1936–), singer

I am so excited about Canadians ruling the world.

–John G. Diefenbaker (1895–1979), prime minister

After feeling for more than a century that being Canadian was a journey rather than a destination, we have arrived at last. We have attained a state of delicious grace which allows us to appreciate that what's important is not so much who we are but that we are—that sometimes a large nation can become a great one.

–Peter C. Newman (1929–), writer

Wherever you go in the world, you just have to say you're Canadian and people laugh.

–John Candy (1950–94), comedian and actor

I think there are tremendous virtues within the country and I personally am more at home with the somewhat reserved, quieter Canadian spirit than with the more energetic American spirit, and being Canadian I therefore understand the wish to preserve it. But I don't think that you necessarily preserve it by keeping those who didn't happen to be born here out of the country.

–Glenn Gould (1932–82), pianist

Canada is…the cry of the loon, Gretzky worship, rye and ginger in a paper cup, vinegar on the fries and…talking gas pumps.

–Nancy White, singer and satirist

Canada has an aboriginal past, a bilingual present, and a multicultural future.

–Gary Filmon (1942–), Manitoba premier

Let me be clear: Canada is not up for grabs. Either you have a country or you don't. You can't have it both ways. My country is Canada. I intend to strengthen it and I intend to keep it.

–Brian Mulroney (1939–), prime minister

As we enter our centennial year we are still a young nation, very much in the formative stages. Our national condition is still flexible enough that we can make almost anything we wish of our nation. No other country is in a better position than Canada to go ahead with the evolution of a national purpose devoted to all that is good and noble and excellent in the human spirit.

–Lester B. Pearson (1897–1972), prime minister

Canada is a country whose main exports are hockey players and cold fronts. Our main imports are baseball players and acid rain.

–Pierre Elliott Trudeau (1919–2000), prime minister

Canada has been the inspiration of my life. I have had before me as a pillar of fire by night and a pillar of cloud by day, a policy of true Canadianism, of moderation, of conciliation…In all the difficulties, all the pains, and all the vicissitudes of our situation, let us always remember that love is better than hatred, and faith better than doubt, and let hope in our future destinies be the pillar of fire to guide us in our career.

–Sir Wilfrid Laurier (1841–1919), prime minister

Canadians must take heed of what they really are in terms of their past, and their northern land. Only then can they find, through their wholeness, the true path to their future.

–Robertson Davies (1913–95), writer

One nation, two cultures; one nationality, two races; one loyalty, two tongues, on this the Dominion of Canada is founded, on this the partnership rests by solemn contract, but mutual trust. And this it must abide or perish.

–Graham Spry (1900–83), nationalist

Canada is not a national state in the usually accepted sense, but a mutable and often dynamic political continuum suited to the varied historical roots of its people and to the broken patterns of its geography. Any attempt to tidy it up into a centralized nation-state would bring its immediate disintegration.

–George Woodcock (1912–95), writer

This country is a land of small towns and big dreams.

–Brian Mulroney (1939–), prime minister

Among the mainstays of my faith is the notion that it is essential to preserve the relatively gentle society on this side of the 49th Parallel. We must reject the seductive but fatal assumption at the source of the American way of life: the gospel that more is better and that progress, efficiency, and monetary gain should be the ultimate goals of human activity. It ain't necessarily so.

–Peter C. Newman (1929–), writer

As they say, you can take the boy out of the country but you can't take the country out of the boy. In my case the country is Canada.

–Leslie Nielsen (1926–), Regina-born actor

We're called upon to reflect on the meaning of what it is to be a Canadian and it's hard to find the usual and common characteristics of historical nations. Certainly we're not united by any particular geography: there are no natural boundaries or very few natural boundaries which define our country. We're not all of us linked by a common history. Many Canadians—almost a third of them—have a very recent history as Canadians. They come with their traditions, their hopes and their beliefs from many parts of the world. And we're not united by one race, one ethnic origin—we're not even united by one language.

–Pierre Elliott Trudeau (1919–2000), prime minister

Because of this movement and change, I think of Canada now as a river. A river is always changing and becoming something else. If you watch what is happening to Toronto you are going to get a picture of what is happening to all Canada and how it will move over the next 50 years. Canada is on the threshold of becoming something else, and that is good. When a country ceases to keep becoming something, it is on the way down.

–Morley Callaghan (1903–90), writer

The term "eh?"—pronounced like a long A—is usually affixed to every sentence out of a Canadian's mouth, from the sublime ("I love you, eh?") to the ridiculous ("Let's get married, eh?") and everything in between ("Gimme a pack of Export, eh?").

–Allan Gould (1944–), journalist and lecturer

WHAT FRIENDS SAY ABOUT ONE ANOTHER

There's our sibling rivalry with our neighbours to the south.

Be realistic about America. Be realistic about Canada; we are a minority shareholder and we have the inevitable options of the minority shareholder—the limited powers of persuasion and the unfathomable powers of prayer.

–Dalton Camp (1920–2002), columnist

We Canadians, as I wrote in the *Spectator* years ago, are the English-speaking world's elected squares. To the British, we are the nicest, whitest Americans. To Americans, we represent a nostalgia for the unhurried horse and buggy age.

–Mordecai Richler (1931–2001), writer

Canada's 5000-mile borderline is unfortified and has the effect of keeping Canadians in a perpetual philosophic mood which nourishes flexibility in the absence of strong commitments or definite goals.

–Marshall McLuhan (1911–80), educator and media philosopher

Canada, today, seems to be "enjoying"—if that is the word—a "love-hate" relationship with the United States.

–W. Earle Mclaughlin, politician, in 1970

The United States is our friend whether we like it or not.

–Robert Thompson (1914–97), Social Credit politician, in 1967

The only thing we are really sure of is that we are not Americans.

–Pierre Berton (1920–2004), writer

I am a Chinese Wall protectionist. I don't mean merely in trade. I mean everything. I'd keep American ideas out of this country.

–Sir William Van Horne (1843–1915), railway builder and capitalist

Canada is dependent on the United States for its culture, its economy, its defence, and its baby alligators. In contrast, the only thing that the States really needs from Canada is water. Some U.S. senators believe that if a way can be found to rid Canada of its impurities (the Canadian people), the country has a tremendous potential as a reservoir.

–Eric Nicol (1919–), humorist and writer

Perhaps the most striking thing about Canada is that it is not part of the United States.

–J. Bartlet Brebner (1895–1957), historian

There is really no anti-Americanism here as far as I can see. The American business manager can go to the golf club or anywhere else. Some people actually look up to the guy: they think he must know more because he's an American. It's a curious Canadian hang-up.

–Max Saltsman (1921–85), politician, in 1971

Americans should never underestimate the constant pressure on Canada which the mere presence of the United States has produced. We're different people from you and we're different people because of you. Living next to you is in some ways like sleeping with an elephant. No matter how friendly and even-tempered is the beast, if I can call it that, one is affected by every twitch and grunt. It should not therefore be expected that this kind of nation, this Canada, should project itself as a mirror image of the United States.

–Pierre Elliott Trudeau (1919–2000), prime minister

After all, we fought the Yanks in 1812 and kicked them the hell out of our country—but not with blanks.

–Farley Mowat (1921–), naturalist and writer

The U.S. is our trading partner, our neighbour, our ally and our friend...and sometimes we'd like to give them such a smack!

–Rick Mercer (1969–), actor

I'm not an American! I am a Canadian. I come from a "nice," thoroughly unrealistic country.

–Matthew Fisher (1947–), organist and singer-songwriter

Canadians have an abiding interest in surprising those Americans who have historically made little effort to learn about their neighbour to the North.

–Peter Jennings (1938–2005), broadcast journalist

Living next door to the United States is like swimming with a whale. You risk being swallowed alive.

–David Peterson (1943–), Ontario premier

When we look at the Americans, we often do so to seek reassurance about our image of ourselves. Regrettably, when they look at us, they think of stereotypes—the three "M"s: Mounties and Mountains and Molson's. They cannot fathom what we are driving at, especially when we talk of our national identity and express concerns about our culture and sovereignty.

–Allan Gotlieb (1928–), Canadian ambassador

President Reagan has said that this deal represents the fulfillment of the American dream. I can understand that. Let the Americans dream, but we have our own dreams. We dream of an independent and a distinct nation north of the 49th Parallel.

–John Turner (1929–), prime minister

JUST A TAD SELF-DEPRECATING

We Canadians are painfully aware of our flaws and bold enough to share them with the world.

The beaver, which has come to represent Canada as the eagle does the United States and the lion Britain, is a flat-tailed, slow-witted, toothy rodent known to bite off its own testicles or to stand under its own falling trees.

–June Callwood (1924–), writer and social activist

The huge advantage of Canada is its backwardness.

–Marshall McLuhan (1911–80), educator and media philosopher

For some reason, a glaze passes over people's faces when you say Canada.

–Sondra Gotlieb (1936–), writer and activist

Canadians, like their historians, have spent too much time remembering conflicts, crises, and failures. They forgot the great, quiet continuity of life in a vast and generous land. A cautious people learns from its past; a sensible people can face its future. Canadians, on the whole, are both.

–Desmond Morton (1937–), historian and writer

Canadians don't have a very big political lever, we're nice guys.

–Paul Henderson (1943–), hockey player

The beginning of Canadian cultural nationalism was not "Am I really that oppressed?" but "Am I really that boring?"

–Margaret Atwood (1939–), writer

Where Canadians got the monotone that you're listening to now I don't know—probably from the Canada goose.

–Northrop Frye (1912–91), literary philosopher

Probably because of our ancient, self-imposed status as a branch-plant country well back in the baggage train of the Anglo-Americans, we have come to regard achievements, other than by professional athletes and geriatrics, as somehow un-Canadian.

–Conrad Black (1944–), media mogul

Whenever I'm away from Canada, the thing I miss most is the apathy.

–Joe Mendelson (1944–), performer and painter

The Canadians knew themselves to be strangers in their own land, without being at home anywhere else.

–Robertson Davies (1913–95), writer

What is a Canadian? Well, the political answer is that he is an American who avoided Revolution.

–Northrop Frye (1912–91), literary philosopher

If Canadians have any claim to international distinction it is because, dull and introverted and all the rest of it though we may be, we have as a people a national gift for tolerance and an acquired skill at compromise.

–Richard Gwyn (1934–), columnist

A Canadian is a D.P. with seniority.

–Dave Broadfoot (1925–), comedian and writer

Canada is seen by some as a confederation of shopping centres.

–Attributed to Pierre Elliott Trudeau (1919–2000), prime minister

I feel that directly in front of us lies a primary need for what I shall call Reconfederation and which I think of essentially as providing a cultural skeleton for the country that fits its present conditions. Without a cultural Reconfederation there can be only continued political tinkering of the most futile kind.

–Northrop Frye (1912–91), literary philosopher

A Canadian is lost when he asks himself what a Canadian is.

–V.S. Pritchett (1900–97), English essayist

Canada has no identity and never has had an identity. Any sense of identity we have is our sense of destiny.

–Marshall McLuhan (1911–80), educator and media philosopher

Canada is not so much a country as a clothesline nearly 4000 miles long. St. John's in Newfoundland is closer to Milan, Italy, than to Vancouver.

–Simon Hoggart (1946–), British journalist

One by one, we can create the sum of our national identity. Canada is a collection of 26 million characters in search of an author.

–Peter C. Newman (1929–), writer

In all that makes a people great, the bounty of nature and the industry of man seem to have combined to ensure for her a noble future. One element alone seems wanting—the cultivation of a national spirit.

–Unsigned editorial in *The Nation*, April 1874

THEN THERE'S THE WEATHER

In the winter there's either too much snow for the city slicker or not enough for the alpine skier. Summers are either so hot that Toronto is under constant smog alerts, or it's so cool your sweater is never far away. And weather is so fickle in the Queen Charlotte Islands that residents there have a saying— "If you don't like the weather, just wait 15 minutes." One thing is certain, though, if you love experiencing weather you'll love to live in Canada!

WINTER

I am told that the Inuit have some 60 words for snow...for different kinds of snow. That does not surprise me. They see a lot of it. I live considerably south of the treeline, but even I have 17 words for snow—none of them useable in public.

–Arthur Black (1943–), broadcaster and writer

Though the Canadian winter does have its disadvantages, it also has its charms. After a day or two of heavy snow the sky brightens, and the air becomes exquisitely clear and free from vapour; the smoke ascends in tall spiral columns till it is lost: seen against the saffron-tinted sky of an evening, or early of a clear morning, when the hoar-frost sparkles on the trees, the effect is singularly beautiful.

–Catharine Parr Traill (1802–99), Ontario pioneer and writer

Man wants but little here below zero.

–"Eye-Opener Bob" Edwards (1864–1922), pioneer journalist

With the thermometer at 30 degrees below zero and the wind behind him, a man walking on Main Street, Winnipeg, knows which side of him is which.

–Stephen Leacock (1869–1944), humorist and writer

I wouldn't say it's cold, but every year Winnipeg's athlete of the year is an ice fisherman.

–Dale Tallon, U.S. journalist, in *Sports Illustrated* on December 22, 1986

THE OTHER TWO MONTHS OF THE YEAR

It was so dry in Saskatchewan during the Depression that the trees were chasing the dogs.

–John Diefenbaker (1895–1979), prime minister

"Cottage" has long been synonymous with "summer" in Canada, but I have found each season at the cottage, or cabin, brings its own delight.

–Roy MacGregor (1948–), writer

I no longer wonder that the elegant arts are unknown here; the rigor of the climate suspends the very powers of the understanding.

–Frances Brooke (1724–1789), British writer

Canadians are careful. We have two railroads, two airlines, two languages, and two temperatures.

–Barry Mather, writer and parliamentarian, in a letter dated July 1, 1979

Anyone who foretells Alberta weather is either a newcomer or a fool.

–Frank Oliver (1853–1933), politician

As for the media, if they can't even tell the truth about the weather, how can they tell the truth about anything else?

–Louis Dudek (1918–2001), poet

I came from the West. And we have a wind there called the chinook. It's a warm wind that pushes back the cold. I'm a chinook.

–Joe Clark (1939–), prime minister, when he was Opposition Conservative leader, in 1976

We need spring. We need it desperately and, usually, we need it before God is willing to give it to us.

–Peter Gzowski (1934–2002), broadcaster and journalist

Spring is not seen, but heard, in Alberta. Drive off the four-lane highway, off the asphalt and onto a gravel road, and stop at the edge of a slough to listen.

–Robert Kroetsch (1927–), writer

MORE THAN JUST THE FROZEN NORTH

Despite what people from other countries might think, Canada is more than just a rugged, frozen wasteland of snow and ice. We've got it all—mountains, rivers, some of the largest freshwater lakes in the world, prairies and deserts. We're surrounded on three sides by ocean, and yes, we have the frozen tundra of the North. But one of Canada's striking features is its immense size occupied by a relatively small population.

TOO MUCH GEOGRAPHY

One of the derivations proposed for the word Canada is a Portuguese phrase meaning "nobody here." The etymology of the word Utopia is very similar, and perhaps the real Canada is an ideal with nobody in it.

–Northrop Frye (1912–91), literary philosopher

If some countries have too much history, we have too much geography.

–William Lyon Mackenzie King (1874–1950), prime minister

If the Canadian people are to find their soul, they must seek for it not in the English language or the French, but in the little ports of the Atlantic provinces, in the flaming autumn maples of the St. Lawrence valley, in the portages and lakes of the Canadian Shield, in the sunsets and relentless cold of the Prairies, in the foothill, mountain and sea of the West and in the unconquerable vastness of the North. From the land, Canada, must come the soul of Canada.

–Arthur Reginald Marsden (A.R.M.) Lower (1889–1988), historian and sailor

The Landless Man to the Manless Land.

–Robert Forke, slogan when serving as Minister of Immigration and Colonization, 1926–29

Canada is big—preposterously so. How can 26 million people lay convincing claim to sovereignty over 3.8 million square miles of a crowded planet?

–F. Kenneth Hare (1919–2002), geographer and climatologist, in 1988

"She's flat, boy," he told me. "This country's flat enough so's you stand on a gopher hill you can see nigh off to China." I believed him, and I still do—for geographers to the contrary, there is no limit to man's vision of those broad plains.

–Farley Mowat (1921–), naturalist and writer

The most characteristic Canadian thing is the Canadian landscape.

–Paul West (1930–), British writer

God knows there's plenty of earth for all of us!
Then why must we sweat for it, deny for it
Pray for it, cry for it
Kill, maim and lie for it
Struggle and suffer and die for it —
We who are gentle and sane?

–Lloyd Roberts (1884–1966), poet

No European except for a Russian can ever take in the size of Canada except by travelling by train. A long plane journey gives some idea, particularly at night when the lights of cities are like rafts in what seems to be the emptiest and darkest of seas.

–Mavis Gallant (1922–), writer

It is a staggering statistic that half of all the fresh water in the world is to be found in Canada.

–Eric W. Morse (1926–95), writer and naturalist

Calgary is surely the only major North American city where, as reflection of its cow-town past, auto expressways are still called Trails.

–John M. Scott, editor of *The Canadian Journey: Rivers of Memory, Rivers of Dreams* (1980)

But always, the farmer, the land, the persistent west wind fiddling on the telephone wire, the towering formulations of cloud. The land. Their heritage. This is what it is all about. Nothing more. The earth and its people.

–Barry Broadfoot (1926–2003), historian and writer

TAKING IT ALL IN

Never at a loss for something to say, writers throughout the ages have been prolific in expressing the beauty of the Canadian wilderness.

What wilderness should be doing is speaking to our souls and teaching us about being quiet...and respecting the world we live in.

–Bill Mason (1929–88), artist and writer

Hudson Bay is certainly a country that Sinbad the Sailor never saw, as he makes no mention of Musketoes.

–David Thompson (1771–1857), geographer, map-maker and explorer

For myself, though I can easily enter into the feelings of the poet and the enthusiasm of the lover of the wild and the wonder of historic lore, I can yet make myself very happy and contented in this country. If its volume of history is yet a blank that of Nature is open, and eloquently marked by the finger of God; and from its pages I can extract a thousand sources of amusement and interest whenever I take my walks in the forest or by the borders of the lakes.

–Catharine Parr Traill (1802–99), Ontario pioneer and writer

From the top of a high rock I had a fine view of the most extensive and dreariest wilderness I have ever beheld. It chilled the heart to gaze on these barren lands of Labrador.

–John James Audubon (1785–1851), naturalist and artist, in 1833

But probably the happiest of all fishermen is the one who rows into the lake far enough to be unobserved, drops anchor, drops a line, and drops off to sleep. All he catches is the sun and his bites are all mosquito, but in the gentle roll of this boat, under the blue sky, the fisherman finds the peace that comes only with exclusion of the rest of the world.

–Eric Nicol (1919–), humorist and writer

I believe a chance to see wildlife under natural conditions is one of the important rights of man. It is a real enrichment of living.

–Roderick Haig-Brown (1908–76), naturalist and writer

I have to say here that Canadian literature, coast to coast, is literally squirming with fish. I could have done a whole anthology of fish stories alone. Seems they're as important in the minds of writers as they are in those of government negotiators, a rare overlap.

–Margaret Atwood (1939–), writer

The happiest man is he who has cultivated to the utmost the sense of beauty. The man who is able at all times to find perfect and prolonged satisfaction in the contemplation of a tree, a field, a flower, or a "spear of grass," can never be bored save by his fellow creatures.

–Archibald Lampman (1861–99), poet

At the heart of all my findings I have discovered a truth more vital and enduring than any captive's experiences in the ominous wilderness. It is the indomitable strength of the human spirit endlessly in search of freedom.

–James Houston (1921–), Native art specialist

One morning, with the snow falling so fat and thick and soft it muffled our coming, I chanced upon four deer here in the clearing. They stared at me and the dog with eyes dark as death, raised their white tails and simply vanished, so soundlessly the poor old dog, her snout buried in the light snow in search of Lord knows what, never even noticed they had been there.

–Roy MacGregor (1948–), writer

I think canoe trips are a bit like childbirth—better remembered than lived through.

–Arthur Black (1943–), broadcaster and writer

Behind me I had the power of 10,000 miles of wilderness, trees that have never told a lie, though some of them have stood for 2000 years.

–Grey Owl (born Archibald Belaney) (1888–1938),
naturalist and writer

PUTTING THE LAND TO WORK

Our country's natural resources are as vast as Canada itself. When it comes to food, our Prairies have been called the bread-basket of the world. Canadian lumber makes its way around the world. We have some of the most prolific oilfields in the world. And the U.S. can't get enough of our hydroelectric power. Rich? You bet we are.

There is a profound attachment to the land rooted in the Canadian character. Farming is the single most important factor in the Canadian experience.

–Allan Anderson, broadcaster and oral historian, in 1977

Let a man get filled up with wheat, and you could get nothing else into him, tho' you offered him heaven.

–Charles W. Gordon (1860–1937), Presbyterian clergyman and novelist under pen name Ralph Connor

There are no happier nor more contented people in the world than the agricultural population of Canada.

–Goldwin Smith, historian, by Charles Edward Whitcombe in *The Canadian Farmer's Manual of Agriculture* (1874)

When there is too much sun, they complain. When there is too much rain, they complain. A farmer is a complainer.

–Pierre Elliott Trudeau (1919–2000), prime minister, in 1979

Between 1890 and 1911 Massey-Harris made 15 per cent of all the manufactured goods exported from Canada. The sun never set on fields where Massey-Harris binders were working.

–Michael Bliss (1941–), historian and writer

Angling is the name given to fishing by people who can't fish.

–Stephen Leacock (1869–1944), humorist and writer

There is nothing disgraceful about being hewers of wood and drawers of water if that is where you find your competitive advantage.

–James Gillies (1924–), politician, in 1977

There is no appearance of venerable antiquity in the Canadian woods. There are no ancient spreading oaks that might be called the patriarchs of the forest. A premature decay seems to be their doom. They are uprooted by the storm, and sink in their first maturity, to give place to a new generation that is ready to fill their places.

–Catharine Parr Traill (1802–99), Ontario pioneer and writer

Let's cut down the trees and create jobs.

–William Vander Zalm (1934–), premier of BC

So, with an average income of well over $6400 a year, as of 1986, Newfoundlanders who…stay on the Rock can make a pretty good living. If they catch some fish on the side. If fishing is their main occupation, though, they've got big problems.

–Allan Gould (1944–), journalist and lecturer

Lord, Please Send Me Another Oil Boom and I Promise I Won't Piss It Away.

–Message on an Albertan bumper sticker, 1987

It is high time that the great resources of nature be used not to make the few rich, but to make the many wise.

–Alfred Fitzpatrick, founded Frontier College in 1899

Fort McMurray seems an unlikely place to go looking for a glimpse into Canada's future....A significant part of Canada's future is now unfolding here in the isolated forests and river valleys of northeastern Alberta.

–Larry Pratt (1944–), political scientist, in 1976

Don't forget, though, we are enjoying resources today which our grandfathers didn't even know existed. Similarly, our grandchildren will probably draw on resources which we don't know exist.

–Jerry McAfee, president of Gulf Oil Canada Limited, in 1975

NOT AS RENEWABLE AS ONCE THOUGHT

*Everyone has a view about how to be a good steward of the land.
Just ask a logger in northern British Columbia.
Chances are he'll point out that the logging industry
diligently replants in the areas that are logged.
Then, of course, there's the fishing industry...*

It is well to remember that there are no new forests to be found. All are known. From here to eternity Canadians must do with what they have.

–G. Herbert Lash (1894–1966), horticulturist and writer

Canada, which supplies almost all the world's newsprint, cuts down 247,000 acres per year more trees than it replants.

–Marjorie Lamb, writer, in 1990

Canadians are lucky people. Nature's lottery has left us with abundant natural resources, oil and gas among them. But we are also a careless people. Rich in resources, we have been poor in policy. And nowhere, perhaps, have we been quite so poor as in our stewardship of the irreplaceable gas and oil reserves that are vital to the well-being of all people in Canada.

–David Crane, columnist, in 1982

Genetic diversity, in both human and non-human species, is a precious planetary resource, and it is in our best interests to monitor and preserve that diversity.

–David Suzuki (1936–),
environmentalist, scientist and media personality

Land is not something you inherit from your parents. It is something you borrow from your children.

–Elmer MacKay (1936–), politician

As a species, our sense of belonging in nature, our sense of place in nature, has been utterly destroyed…This is the unilateral divorce from life and living that is the unique accomplishment of our condition.

–John A. Livingston, Canadian naturalist, in 1981

Removing the earth's nonrenewable resources, no matter how urgent and necessary, is an emotional business and it is natural that people should hold strong feelings on this subject. Add to that a succession of sizeable price increases for petroleum products—most of which go to governments, incidentally—and you have a real firecracker on your hands.

–J.A. Armstrong, past chairman of the board of Imperial Oil, speaking to shareholders in 1976

This land is far more important than we are. To know it is to be young and ancient all at once.

–Hugh MacLennan (1907–90), writer

The struggle that has formed our national character has not been a contest between other people but against the elements, against the cold and the wind and the stubborn rock. This is a clean battle, but it yields no victories, only the postponement of defeats.

–Peter C. Newman (1929–), writer

Anything which speeds up an environment around another environment destroys the environment it surrounds.

–Marshall McLuhan (1911–80), educator and media philosopher

I have been, all my life, what is known as a conservationist. I am not at all sure that this has done myself or anyone else any good, but I am quite sure that no intelligent man, least of all a countryman, has any alternative. It seems clear beyond possibility of argument that any given generation of men can have only a lease, not ownership, of the earth; and one essential term of the lease is that the earth be handed on to the next generation with unimpaired potentialities. This is the conservationist's concern.

–Roderick Haig-Brown (1908–76), naturalist and writer

There's a torn and splintered ridge across the stumps I call the "screamers." These are the unsawn last bits, the cry of the tree's heart, wrenching and tearing apart just before she gives that sway and the dreadful groan of falling, that dreadful pause while her executioners step back with their saws and axes resting and watch....They are their own tombstones and their own mourners.

–Emily Carr (1871–1945), artist and writer

Among the serious problems facing industrial society, none is more acute than the deterioration of our environment.

–Brian Mulroney (1939–), prime minister

In Japan, I was amazed to find that over 50 percent of their solid waste is recycled....If we recycled paper at the same rate as the Japanese, we could save 80 million trees a year—an amount that equals the total annual logging production of Ontario.

–Dave Nichol, president of Loblaws,
speaking at the Summit on the Environment,
Toronto, September 11, 1989

Once it took Haida Indians in the Queen Charlotte Islands more than a year to cut down a single giant cedar. When the Europeans arrived with the technological know-how—the two-man saw and steel ax—the task was shortened to a week. Today, one man with a portable chainsaw can fell that tree in an hour.

–Anita Gordon and David Suzuki (1936–),
science broadcasters, in 1990

There's an old saying which goes: Once the last tree is cut and the last river poisoned, you will find you cannot eat your money.

–Joyce McLean, writer, in *The Globe and Mail*, November 1, 1989

We are like yeast in a vat—mindlessly multiplying as we greedily devour a finite world. If we do not change our ways, we will perish as the yeasts perish—having exhausted our sustenance and poisoned ourselves in the lethal brew of our own wastes.

–Farley Mowat (1921–), naturalist and writer

Life on this Earth is not a democracy. If it were, then by what right has man, the minority, the right to poison the air and the land and to continue on his mad suicide race without heeding the implied desires of all the other living creatures.

–Leslie A. Croutch (1915–69), writer

The dramatic discovery of the century is that the earth, far from being massive, imponderable, and inexhaustible, is small and finite. Man must make himself small and humble to live within it rather than a ruthless giant to conquer it.

–Roderick Haig-Brown (1908–76), naturalist and writer

What we hope to do is to show that one individual, peacefully and non-violently, standing between the gun and the seal, the harpoon and the whale, the factory and the stream, can force his opponent into a decision and can make for change.

–David McTaggart, a founder of Greenpeace, in 1978

One day all too soon there will be nothing left to love.

–Farley Mowat (1921–), naturalist and writer

The North, as has been said more than once, is Canada's last frontier. We need to make sure it does not become Canada's lost frontier by virtue of being taken over—lock, stock and barrel—by the U.S. multinational corporations, in the same way they have taken over other parts of the Canadian economy, with the complicity of federal and provincial governments.

–William Kashtan (1909–93),
leader of the Communist Party of Canada, in 1976

REGIONAL PATRIOTISM

Emily Murphy, Alberta writer,
described Winnipeg with these wondrous words:
"How the sun shines here in Winnipeg!
One drinks it in like wine. And how the bells ring!
It is a town of bells and light set in a blaze of gold."
Music to the ears of a true Prairie lass, but not necessarily a sentiment shared by the folks in Winnipeg in the dead of winter. Still, Canadians are, if nothing else, patriotic to their province.

THE WEST

Canada is like an old cow. The West feeds it. Ontario and Québec milk it. And you can well imagine what it's doing in the Maritimes.

–Tommy Douglas (1904–86),
leader of the NDP; Saskatchewan CCF premier

Winnipeg, Winnipeg, Gateway of the West
Always growing greater, never growing less
Winnipeg, Winnipeg, we are not so slow
We are always boosting, everywhere we go!

–cheer of the Young Men's Section of the Winnipeg Board of Trade

Edmonton isn't really the end of the world—although you can see it from there.

–Ralph Klein (1942–), Alberta premier, when mayor of Calgary

Saint-Boniface breathed, prayed, hoped, sang and suffered in French, but it earned its living in English, in the offices, stores, and factories of Winnipeg. The irremediable and existential difficulty of being French-Canadian in Manitoba or elsewhere.

–Gabrielle Roy (1909–83), writer

No one is born in the Prairies who can help it, and no one dies there who can get out in time.

–Anonymous, 1923

I always feel that I have the right to call myself a Canadian because I am, in a small way, a rancher. I always feel that my small ranch in Alberta is to me a great link with Canada and that it is an assurance that I shall return there some day.

–Prince of Wales (1894–1972), the future Edward VIII, in 1922

I just think you Westerners should take over this country if you are so smart.

–Pierre Elliott Trudeau (1919–2000), prime minister

Winnipeg is the West.

–Rupert Brooke (1887–1915), British poet, in a collection entitled *Letters from America*, published posthumously in 1916

The doors of vast opportunity lay wide open and Canada's adventurous sons flocked to Winnipeg to have a part in the great expansion—the building of a newer and greater Canadian West. They were big men, come together with big purpose. Their ideas were big, and they fought for the realization of them.

–George H. Ham (1847–1926), journalist

To the native of the Prairies, Alberta is the far West; British Columbia the near East.

–Edward A. McCourt (1907–72), writer, in his book *Canada West in Fiction* (1949)

Manitoba is a corruption of two Indian words *Manitou napa*, "the land of the great spirit." The Manitobans translate it more freely as "God's Country."

–Emily Murphy (1868–1933), Alberta judge, social activist and writer

I think of western skies as one of the most beautiful things about the West, and the western horizons. The Westerner doesn't have a point of view. He has a vast panorama; he has such tremendous space around him.

–Marshall McLuhan (1911–80), educator and media philosopher

There are more left-handed Mormon streakers in the West than there are western separatists.

–Mel Hurtig (1932–),
writer; publisher; co-founder of the Council of Canadians

I began to discover the three governing dimensions of the Prairies: the sky, the land, and the loneliness. They reduced a man to less than a cell in this vast breathing organism. Yet, in another sense, he was enlarged and reoriented not only to his own minor planet but to the space and mystery beyond it.

–Bruce Hutchison (1901–92), newspaper editor and author

I had accepted the job at Edmonton in order to return to Canada...But I had not realized how far north Edmonton was. It was a raw city, vibrating with energy, but saddled with what I thought were enormous handicaps—a flat landscape relieved only by the river, mosquitoes as big as sparrows in the summer, and winters that were inhumanly cold.

–David Suzuki (1936–),
environmentalist, scientist and media personality

If I'm asked what my image of Manitoba is, the one that comes to mind spontaneously is that of the giant plain, open, immense, yet tender and full of dreams.

–Gabrielle Roy (1909–83), writer

CENTRAL CANADA

I have married an Englishman, and have made my home in England, but I still remain at heart a French Canadian.

–Emma (Lajeunesse) Albani (1847–1930), international songstress

Ontario is the hardest province to grasp. Partly because of its size and the diversities of its dimensions. And because it represents the standard against which the other regions measure their differences. And because for many, Ontario is Canada.

–Heather Menzies (1949–), writer

Two things hold this country together. Everybody hates Air Canada coffee, and everybody hates Ontario.

–Brian Peckford (1942–), Newfoundland premier, in 1979

This province is a country within a country. Québec the original heart. The hardest and deepest kernel. The core of first time. All around, nine other provinces form the flesh of this still-bitter fruit called Canada.

–Anne Hebert (1916–2000), writer

Without Québec, Canada wouldn't have any heart and Canadian life would cease.

–Pierre Elliott Trudeau (1919–2000), prime minister

We are Québeckers. What it means above all else is that we are attached only to this corner of the world where we can be fully ourselves.

–René Lévesque (1922–87), Québec premier

Even before the flattest Québec landscape I feel that I have more to say than before the magnificent sites of Europe.

–John Lyman (1886–1967), artist and critic, in 1927

THE ATLANTIC PROVINCES

For Newfoundlanders living by and upon it, the sea is the ultimate reality. They accept it as their master, for they know they will never master it. The sea is there. It is their destiny. It gives them life, and sometimes it gives them death.

–Farley Mowat (1921–), naturalist and writer

The *Bluenose* is more than a name—a ship or a service. It contains in its eight letters something of the heart and life that flows by the waters of Minas, Fundy and the restless Atlantic. It designates a people—and lives in their blood.

–Henry D. Hicks, Nova Scotia premier, in 1959

Down in Newfoundland, we can hardly sleep for wondering when St. Pierre and Miquelon are going to invade.

–John Crosbie (1931–), politician

The calamities of the Maritimes have always been casually passed along as acts of God, over which governments have no responsibility; while apparently, from the official point of view Divinity does not operate in other sectors of Canada.

–J.J. Hayes Doone (1888–1953), senator

With a Polish pope and a Newfie finance minister, you mainlanders had better watch your jokes.

–John Crosbie (1931–), politician

Politics in Newfoundland have never been such as to inspire wholehearted confidence in the ability of the people to govern themselves wisely, but there is general agreement that a process of deterioration, which has now reached almost unbelievable extremes, may be said to have set in about a quarter of a century ago.

–From the *Newfoundland Royal Commission Report* for Great Britain, dated 1933

THE NORTH

The Arctic is a world, not of Man, scarcely of beast, but of physical and geological and meteorological attributes only; it belongs to the universe of first creation, but not to the universe of last creation; of the First and Second Days, not of the Sixth Day.

–Kenneth P. Kirkwood, author and diplomat, between 1940 and 1943

The North is the only place where Nature can still claim to rule, the only place as yet but little vexed by man. All over the globe there spread his noisy failures; the North alone is silent and at peace. Give man time and he will spoil that too.

–Stephen Leacock (1869–1944), humorist and writer

One of the best things about the North is that once you have been there, not only the memories but also the friends you meet there stay with you forever. It is like joining a special club as a lifetime member, and you never quite get over a longing to go back.

–Edith Iglauer (1917–), journalist

The more I see of the country, the less I feel I know about it. There is a saying that after five years in the North every man is an expert; after 10 years, a novice.

–Pierre Berton (1920–2004), writer

THROUGH THE EYES OF THE ARTIST

Whether working with found objects or a pen and paper, art is the ability to envision something beautiful and breathe life into that image. It is incumbent upon the person with such a gift to share it with—and challenge—the world around him. English philosopher Herbert Read wrote, "The worth of a civilization or a culture is not valued in the terms of its material wealth or military power, but by the quality and achievements of its representative individuals—its philosophers, its poets, and its artists." If that is so, Canada is very rich indeed.

ART IS AN ACT OF FAITH

Artists, the real ones, the committed ones, have always sought, sometimes in ways prophetic and beyond their own times, to clarify and proclaim and enhance life, not to obscure and demean and destroy it. Even the so-called literature of despair is not really that at all. Despair is total silence, total withdrawal. Art, by its very nature of necessary expression, is an act of faith, an acknowledgement of the profound mystery at the core of life.

–Margaret Laurence (1926–87), writer

Here was symbolized, it came to me, the function of the artist in life: he must accept in deep singleness of purpose the manifestations of life in man and in nature, and transform these into controlled, ordered and vital expressions of meaning.

–Lauren Harris (1885–1970), artist and member of the Group of Seven

Literature is conscious mythology: as society develops, its mythical stories become structural principles of storytelling, its mythical concepts, sun-gods and the like, become habits of metaphoric thought. In a fully mature literary tradition the writer enters into a structure of traditional stories and images.

–Northrop Frye (1912–91), literary philosopher

The Group of Seven artists whose pictures are here exhibited have for several years held a like vision concerning Art in Canada. They are all imbued with the idea that an Art must grow and flower in the land before the country will be a real home for its people.

–From the catalogue for the Group of Seven's first art exhibition, May 1920

Like every other form of art, literature is no more and nothing less than a matter of life and death. The only question worth asking about a story—or a poem, or a piece of sculpture, or a new concert hall—is, "is it dead or alive?" If a work of the imagination needs to be coaxed into life, it is better scrapped and forgotten.

–Mavis Gallant (1922–), writer

The people do not exist for the sake of art, to give the painter fame or the picture a market. On the contrary, art exists for the sake of the people, to refresh the weary, to console the sad, to increase man's joy of living and his sympathies with all the world.

–Madge Young Clement,
singer and first president of The Brandon Art Club

Women, as well as men, in all ages and in all places, have danced on the earth, danced the life dance, danced joy, danced grief, danced despair, and danced hope. Literally danced all these and more, and danced them figuratively and metaphorically, by their very lives.

–Margaret Laurence (1926–87), writer

We also came to realize that we in Canada cannot truly understand the great cultures of the past and of other peoples until we ourselves commence our own creative life in the arts. Until we do so, we are looking at these from the outside.

–Lauren Harris (1885–1970), artist and member of the Group of Seven

In the only address that I made, I said that I thought of the writers of this country as being members of a kind of tribe…there is still that tremendous sense of belonging to a community. And we all need that sense of community.

–Margaret Laurence (1926–87), writer

Music is a universal language, and the only one, crossing all borders, arising in all cultures, closely allied to them, understood and employed in the most primitive as well as the most advanced. In our day superficial fashions come and go, hastened by the swift communications of modern technology, but the permanence of the great musical classics remains solid and untarnished.

–J. Francis Leddy (1911–98), educator

WHAT IS ART?

The meaning of art, like the meaning of life, is always in flux. There are as many opinions about what it is and what makes great art as there are artists and art lovers.

Art is anything that people do with distinction.

–Louis Dudek (1918–2001), poet

The exercise of creative power inevitably produces instability, conflict and confusion, for when man is creative he is always in private or open opposition to the established order.

–Carlyle King (1907–88), university professor

Art can never be understood, but can only be seen as a kind of magic, the most profound and mysterious of all human activities.

–Bill Reid (1920–98), Haida artist

To me, the most important thing in a piece of art is the thought. Technique is totally secondary.

–Robert Bateman (1930–), artist

Pain is temporary. Film is forever.

–Michael J. Fox (1961–), actor

The artist is, after all, the universe's crowning achievement, matter becoming fully aware of itself.

–Irving Layton (1912–2006), poet

We have as little desire to be revolutionary as to be old-fashioned. The painter must rely on paint and not on adjectives.

–From the catalogue for the Group of Seven's second art exhibition, May 1921

Creative Art is "fresh seeing." Why, there is all the difference between copying and creating that there is between walking down a hard straight cement pavement and walking down a winding grassy lane with flowers peeping everywhere and the excitement of never knowing what is just around the next bend!

–Emily Carr (1871–1945), writer and artist

Songs are thoughts, sung out with the breath when people are moved by great forces and ordinary speech no longer suffices. Man is moved just like the ice floe sailing here and there out in the current. His thoughts are driven by a flowing force when he feels joy, when he feels fear, when he feels sorrow.

–Orpingalik, Inuit singer, in 1970

Write the truth, for that is what makes literature.

–George M. Wrong (1860–1948), historian

The book is the world's most patient medium.

–Northrop Frye (1912–91), literary philosopher

There is no such thing as Indian art, only Indian artists.

–Del Ashkewe (1947–), Native spokesperson

I would rather be on the governing board of the Canadian Radio Corporation than on the board of the greatest university in the world, for radio is the greatest university. Everyone belongs to it—and no one can be excluded because they have not passed.

–Nellie McClung (1873–1951), writer, activist and Alberta MLA

Ballet on the Prairies was only something in the memory of many Canadians who had come from Europe at the beginning of the century, a lingering dream of colour and movement almost lost in the years of achievement and hardship in a new country.

–Gweneth Lloyd, co-founder of the Royal Winnipeg Ballet, in 1975

ONE OF A KIND

Everyone's style in his or her preferred medium is personal. No two artists, like no two snowflakes, are alike.

Style! I have no style, I merely wait till the mud settles.

–Goldwin Smith (1823–1910), writer and editor

I only write books about dead people. They can't sue.

–Pierre Berton (1920–2004), writer and media personality

I wanted to develop the idea of torch and twang, that's what's inside me and it pretty much sums up the kind of music that interests me.

–k.d. lang (1961–), singer, in 1989

I skate the way I think Isadora Duncan danced. I'm trying to explore every facet of my personality. I'm criticized as flamboyant, arrogant, and melodramatic. I'm black and white. I'm yes and no. I try to live my life touching extremes.

–Toller Cranston (1949–), figure skater

It just seemed an absolute natural; the city by the name of Stratford, on the river by the name of Avon, with the lovely park system. What's more natural than a Shakespearean Festival?

–Tom Patterson (1921–2005), founder of the Stratford Festival

I suppose history has taught me this: every person has an individual story. The stories have similar patterns, but each is unique and particular…One of the beautiful things about telling stories is that you never tell them completely.

–Rudy Wiebe (1934–), writer

ALL THAT ATTITUDE

Never let it be said an artist is a wallflower! They are typically temperamental, blunt, perceptive, sensitive, occasionally irritable and always on the lookout for inspiration. Being a writer or musician or painter or actor isn't just a way to earn a meagre living, it's a vocation, a calling—it's who you are.

I've also seen that great men are often lonely. This is understandable, because they have built such high standards for themselves that they often feel alone. But that same loneliness is part of their ability to create.

–Yousuf Karsh (1908–2002), photographer and journalist

We must not make bosses of our intellectuals. And we do them no good by letting them run the arts. Should they, when they read novels, find nothing in them but the endorsement of their opinions? Are we here on Earth to play such games?

–Saul Bellow (1915–2005), writer

No greater curse can befall a man than to be afflicted with artistic leanings in Canada.

–Frederick Philip Grove (1879–1948), novelist

After my husband died I felt very alone and unwanted; making prints is what has made me happiest since he died. I am going to keep on doing them until they tell me to stop. If no one tells me to stop, I shall make them as long as I am well. If I can, I'll make them even after I am dead.

–Pitseolak Ashoona (1904–83), Inuit artist

Authors like cats because they are such quiet, lovable wise creatures, and cats like authors for the same reason.

–Robertson Davies (1913–95), writer

If I'm not back in five minutes…just wait longer!

–Jim Carrey (1962–), actor

One must try to be as objective as possible. The human face masks the true nature of the individual. I would like to think if I had photographed Hitler that the bestiality and ruthlessness would have shown through. I would not deliberately try for the inhumanity—and you can. It would have just come out.

–Yousuf Karsh (1908–2002), photographer and journalist

The poet is like a cocoon; in him the caterpillar of the past finds rest, and from him the butterfly of the future emerges.

–A.M. Klein (1909–72), poet

The poet has really only two themes and they are Eros and Thanatos and if he lives long enough and thinks hard enough he becomes aware that they are interchangeable or that there is a beneficent tension between them.

–Irving Layton (1912–2006), poet

To make enduring photographs, one must learn to see with one's mind's eyes, for the heart and the mind are the true lens of the camera.

–Yousuf Karsh (1908–2002), photographer and journalist

You never have to change anything you got up in the middle of the night to write.

–Saul Bellow (1915–2005), writer

Character, like a photograph, develops in darkness.

–Yousuf Karsh (1908–2002), photographer and journalist

Artists as a class are the poorest people in the country except for old age pensioners and Native people living on reservations.

–George Woodcock (1912–95), writer

You can't make a film just for the Canadian public; and, often, when you make a film just for the Canadian public, even the Canadian public doesn't want to see it.

–Ivan Reitman (1946–), director

People can lose their lives in libraries. They ought to be warned.

–Saul Bellow (1915–2005), writer

Canadian literature is very interesting so long as you don't bother to read it.

–Louis Dudek (1918–2001), poet

You see, the world is full of beautiful voices, but they're lazy beautiful voices. You've got to be responsible to the talent you start with, and then you can make a career for yourself.

–Riki Turofsky (1944–), opera singer

The only Canadian mythology is that there is a Canadian mythology.

–Irving Layton (1912–2006), poet

For most of my life I have been a student of the world's mythologies, which I have found reveal a truer and fuller vision of the human mind and soul than all the historical, psychological and anthropological studies ever devised.

–David Day, author of *A Tolkien Bestiary*, in 1979

However, unlike Gertrude Stein who wrote, "A rose is a rose is a rose," the Indian would be more likely to say, "A bird is a loon is an eagle is a man is a manitou!"

–Selwyn Dewdney (1909–79), Native art specialist

Once I asked an Indian why the old people disliked so intensely being sketched or photographed, and he replied, "Our old people believe that the spirit of the person becomes enchained in the picture. When they died it would still be held there and could not go free." Perhaps they too were striving to capture the spirit of the totem and hold it there and keep these supernatural beings within close call.

–Emily Carr (1871–1945), artist and writer

In a sense, we haven't got an identity until somebody tells our story. The fiction makes us real.

–Robert Kroetsch (1927–), writer

REMEMBERING THE GREAT ONES

Even though Canadians are often too modest to herald one of their own, greatness is recognized. Sometimes we recognize the contributions of an entire culture, such as the contributions from Canada's First Nations. Other times that recognition is more pointed toward an individual, such as the case of Tom Thomson, the artist credited with inspiring the Group of Seven. Either way, in the arts community all are remembered.

He lived humbly but passionately with the wild. It made him brother to all untamed things of nature. It drew him apart and revealed itself wonderfully to him.

–Inscription on Tom Thomson's cairn

I rather think it would have been wiser to have taken your ten most prominent Canadians and sunk them in Canoe Lake—and saved Tom Thomson.

–David Milne (1882–1953), artist

These Arctic carvings are not the cold sculptures of a frozen world. Instead, they reveal to us the passionate feelings of a vital people well aware of all the joys, terrors, tranquillity, and wilderness of life around them.

–James Houston (1921–), Native art specialist

If he asks for bread, he is offered a tombstone. I always suspect an artist who is successful before he is dead.

–John Murray Gibbon (1875–1952), artist

For 800 years at least, people have been carrying on the art of the Haidas on the islands, and it is that heritage that I have drawn upon. So this pole I would like to dedicate, more than anything else, to the memory of the great carvers and all the people who supported them.

–Bill Reid (1920–98), master carver of the Haidas

FOOD AS ART

While eating is something we have to do to live, those who make their living in the culinary world—and take that calling to a level of expertise—are wont to call themselves artists. Just turn on Food Network Canada and you'll see what I mean.

Much as I enjoy writing and teaching, they box me in. In the kitchen I take wings.

–Madame Jehane Benoit (1904–87), chef and writer

A gourmet is a person who knows and loves food. Forget about the misuse of the word in advertising, and its connotation of the over refined, picky eater. A gourmet, his greed notwithstanding, has a lot to offer Canada. He is a seeker after excellence, and anyone in this country who craves excellence in anything counterbalances a Canadian weakness, the desire for an easy road, at the end of which is mediocrity.

–Sondra Gotlieb (1936–), writer and activist

Chips and vinegar or poutine, butter tarts or tourtiere, dim sum or bagels or chapatti or baklava are *a votre choix.* Where else in the world is all this diversity taken for granted?

–Charles Pachter (1942–) artist, in 1991

Just a little bit of this and a little bit of that.

–Madame Jehane Benoit (1904–87), chef and writer

OUR FIRST NATIONS PEOPLES

How Canada has dealt with its First Nations peoples from the first discovery of this vast land is perhaps the most damning chapter in our history.

ON BEING NATIVE

Who we are is often defined by what we value in the world around us. For Canada's First Nations people, a relationship with nature and a deep abiding respect for the Creator are just a few of those values.

The root of the word "society" is "friendship" and "companionship." This concept is the basis of the Kaienerekowa, the Great Law of Peace, and the Constitution of the Five Nations Iroquois Confederation. The Great Law is a way of life that was given to us as we saw it. It's how we are to relate to the universe, which is the way that I have tried to live.

–Kahn-Tineta Horn (1940–), Mohawk activist

I feel as an Indian, think as an Indian, all my ways are Indian, my heart is Indian. They, more than the whites, are to me, my people.

–Grey Owl (born Archibald Belaney) (1888–1938), naturalist and writer

I'm just an ordinary Indian and I want to remain an ordinary Indian.

–Elijah Harper (1949–), Ojibway-Cree and politician

I looked around at my culture and said what do Indian people need? We need a sense of our own joy, our own beauty, our own dignity, our own life and laughter.

–Buffy Sainte-Marie (1941–), singer and First Nations activist

I am proud to be an Eskimo, but I think we can improve on the igloo as a permanent dwelling.

–Abraham Okpik, Inuit spokesperson, in 1960

We must prove to Canada that the original citizens of this country will not lie down and play dead. After all, the Inuit have been described by the United Nations as a people who refuse to disappear.

–John Amagoalik, Inuit writer, in 1977

We, the original people of this country, have inherited through the oral traditions of our forefathers…distinct original languages. Fifty-two of these original languages of Canada are now on the brink of extinction. Unlike you, we cannot retrieve these languages from our mother country. Our mother country is Canada. What we lose in Canada, we lose forever. We cannot let the voices of our forefathers be silenced forever.

–Phil Fontaine (1944–),
grand chief of the Association of Manitoba Chiefs

The Spirit of God made me realize the extent of the rights which the Indian possesses to the land of the Northwest. Yes, the extent of the Indian rights, the importance of the Indian cause is far above all other interests. People say the Native stands on the edge of a chasm. It is not he who stands on the edge of the chasm; his claims are not false. They are just. The land question will soon be resolved, as it must, to his complete satisfaction. Every step the Indian takes is based upon a profound sense of fairness.

–Louis Riel (1844–85), Métis leader

Don't knock a man down and then ask why he lives in the dirt. Don't strip a man of his clothing and then ask why he is naked. Don't filch a man of his authority, his right to rule his home, his dignity as a man, and then ask him why his culture is substandard.

–Chief Dan George (1899–1981),
First Nations spokesperson, in 1966

HISTORICAL VIEWS OF FIRST NATIONS PEOPLES

Some pioneers were narrow-minded and judgmental. Others took a more objective view of a culture different from their own, and a more critical look at where they came from.

The term person means an individual other than an Indian.

–Section 12 of the Indian Act of 1880

Every Indian or other person who engages in or assists in celebrating the Indian festival known as the "Potlatch" or in the Indian dance known as the "Tamanawas" is guilty of a misdemeanor, and shall be liable to imprisonment for a term of not more than six nor less than two months.

–Indian Act Amendment, 1884

They have good reason to be suspicious, for in the past there have been occasions when a friendly hand from the government turned out to have a knife in it.

–James Gladstone (1887–1971), Canada's first Native senator

Ottawa is trying to make Indians little brown white men.

–Adam Solway, First Nations chief

When we in touch with heathen come
We send them first a case of rum
Next, to rebuke their native sin
We send a missionary in.

–Stephen Leacock (1869–1944), humorist and writer

I want to get rid of the Indian problem. Our object is to continue until there is not a single Indian in Canada that has not been absorbed into the body politic, and there is no Indian question, and no Indian department.

–Duncan Campbell Scott (1862–1947),
when he was deputy superintendent of Indian Affairs, 1913–23

Go to the nearest well-to-do farmer and spend the night in his pigsty (with the pigs of course) and this is exactly life with the Esquimaux.

–William Bompas (1820–1906),
Arctic missionary and Anglican bishop, in 1865

I prefer the Indians on the score of consistency; they are what they profess to be, and we are not what we profess to be. They profess to be warriors and hunters, and are so; we profess to be Christians, and civilized—are we so?

–Anna Brownell Jameson (1794–1860),
English traveller and writer, from her book
Winter Studies and Summer Rambles in Canada (1838)

I have heard and read much of savages, and have since seen, during my long residence in the bush, somewhat of uncivilized life; but the Indian is one of Nature's gentlemen—he never says or does a rude or vulgar thing. The vicious, uneducated barbarians who form the surplus of over populous European countries are far behind the wild man in delicacy of feeling or natural courtesy.

–Susanna Moodie (1803–85), pioneer and writer

They are Crees, their language a pretty one; the astounding thing was to hear them repeat long exercises, such as the creed, sing hymns, read the Testament, etc., in English not one word of which any of them understood.

–John Henry Lefroy (1817–90), British explorer and surveyor

One hardly knows whether to take an Indian as a problem, a nuisance, or a possibility. He may be considered from a picturesque, philanthropic, or pestiferous standpoint, according to your tastes or opportunities. You may idealize him, or realize him.

–Emily Murphy (1868–1933), Alberta judge, social activist and writer

The great themes of Canadian history are as follows: Keeping the Americans out, keeping the French in, and trying to get the Natives to somehow disappear.

–Will Ferguson, writer

CRITICAL VIEWS

Writers, artists and politicians have, through the years, reflected on our nation's downfalls. And Native spokespersons have critiqued Canadian government policy as well as the image projected by some of their own people.

A day-care centre surrounded by red tape, Indian Affairs has always been long on benevolence, but short on beneficence; for further details, ask any of the department's clientele.

–Dalton Camp (1920–2002), columnist

Canada must be the only country in the world where sending in the federal troops to replace police is considered a means of de-escalating tension. Actually, the decision by Québec Premier Robert Bourassa to ask for, and that by Prime Minister Brian Mulroney to agree to, the use of the army at the Oka standoff is a commentary of sorts on how low things have sunk in the country we all used to think could be an example to the world of civilized behaviour.

–Fred Cleverly, writer,
from his column in the *Winnipeg Free Press*, August 13, 1990

If somebody wanted to play golf on my mother's grave, I'd be a little upset.

–Graham Greene (1952–), Iroquois actor

Only a small part of Canada is covered by treaties, about 20%. The white population residing in the rest of Canada had to get their land somehow and you can be sure that very few sought out Native real estate dealers.

–Lloyd Caibaiosai, artist, in 1970

Land Claims—A classic example of Canadian compromise, 50/50, equal rights: the Inuit, Indians and Métis have the claims, the Canadian government keeps the land.

– Allan Gould (1944–), journalist and lecturer

Growing up red is not the same as growing up white; for my people, the real people, the red men, think our own thoughts. We have our own magic, and our own mysteries.

–Alma Greene (1896–1978), Mohawk writer

My culture is like a wounded deer that has crawled away into the forest to bleed and to die alone.

–Chief Dan George (1899–1981),
First Nations spokesperson, in 1974

When you no longer go around accounting for yourself, making yourself understood, justifying your existence, when you no longer feel an alien anywhere, you've come home. You know who you are.

–Wilfred Pelletier (1927–), First Nations educator, in 1973

Why don't you all go back to where you came from?
We own this land; we're your landlords. And the rent is due.

–Kahn-Tineta Horn (1940–), Mohawk activist, in 1969

Native issues are almost never just Native issues. Native issues are human issues.

–Buffy Sainte-Marie (1941–), singer and First Nations activist

I am distressed by the fact that one of the most common visual symbols within the Canadian urban psyche is that of an Indian drunk at every major street corner of every major Canadian city.

–Thomson Highway (1951–), Manitoba-born Cree writer

NATURE AND THE FIRST NATIONS

Traditionally, the First Nations peoples have a unique relationship with nature—a relationship of respect as well as dependence.

Is heaven more beautiful than the country of the muskox in summer when sometimes the mist blows over the lakes, and sometimes the water is blue, and the loons cry very often?

–Saltatha Inuit saying

Our land is more valuable than your money. It will last forever. It will not perish as long as the sun shines and the water flows, through all the years it will give life to men and beasts. It was put there by the Great Spirit and we cannot sell it because it does not belong to us.

–Crowfoot, First Nations chief, in a speech he delivered in the 1870s

Before you whites came to trouble the ground, our rivers were full of fish and our woods of deer. Our creeks abounded with beaver and our plains were covered with buffalo. But now we are brought to poverty. Our beavers are gone for ever; our buffalo have fled to the lands of our enemies...The geese are afraid to pass over the smoke of our chimneys and we are left to starve while you whites grow rich on the dust of our fathers...

–Peguis, First Nations chief, part of his speech delivered in 1817

The heavens snared the storm clouds with the rainbow; the sunshine smiled on the earth. May the heavens snare the warclouds with the rainbow and bless the earth with the sublimity of eternal spiritual values in the brotherhood of men and bring everlasting peace on earth.

–Assiniboine Prayer for Peace

CANADA... STANDING GUARD FOR HUMAN RIGHTS

As a Canadian, I am free.
Canadians should not take their freedom for granted.
It is a gift that brings a quality of life not shared
by everyone in the world. It's a gift that needs protection.

FREEDOM AND EQUALITY

I am a Canadian, a free Canadian
free to speak without fear
free to worship God in my own way
free to stand for what I think right
free to oppose what I believe wrong
free to choose those who shall govern my country.
This heritage of freedom I pledge to uphold
for myself and mankind.

–Preamble to the Canadian Bill of Rights.
adopted by the House of Commons July 1, 1960

I am more convinced than ever that there cannot be a lasting civilization unless it preserves freedom and moves towards equality.

–Stanley Knowles (1908–97), parliamentarian

Political freedom is rare enough in the world, but the kind of social and cultural freedom which is the hallmark of Canada is even less common.

–Joe Clark (1939–), prime minister, when he was an MP in 1977

The freedoms we now share and cherish are equal to the best of countries on this planet. They are surpassed by none. They can be greater still. It is not necessary to break the bonds of our common history to do so.

–Edward R. Schreyer (1935–), governor general of Canada

My allegiance is to ideas, and most especially to the extraordinary idea of individual liberty.

–Barbara Amiel (1940–), columnist

Every person and every class of persons shall enjoy the right to obtain and retain employment without discrimination with respect to the compensation, terms, conditions or privileges of employment because of the race, creed, religion, colour or ethnic or national origin of such person or class of persons.

–from the Saskatchewan Bill of Rights, 1947

To say that all men are equal has not got us very far. It is more accurate to say that all men are different, and then to respect each other's differences.

–Reginald Ruggles Gates (1882–1962), botanist and pioneer geneticist

I had seen their tears and sighs, and I had heard their groans, and I would give every drop of blood in my veins to free them.

–Harriet Ross Tubman (1820–1913),
activist in the campaign to abolish U.S. slavery

Every child a wanted child, every mother a willing mother.

–Henry Morgentaler (1923–), physician and pro-choice advocate

The freedom of no one is safe unless the freedom of everyone is safe.

–Motto of the Canadian Civil Liberties Association,
established in Toronto in 1964

Freedom is the right to be wrong, not to do wrong.

–John G. Diefenbaker (1895–1979), prime minister

Speech is not free now and never has been free and never will be free. Freedom of speech only exists in proportion to indifference to the thing spoken of.

–Stephen Leacock (1869–1944), humorist and writer

NOBODY'S BABY

In the 21st century, little girls are welcomed into a world where possibilities for their future are unlimited. It's not just about "sugar and spice and all things nice" anymore. Today, girls can aspire to become doctors, to explore outer space, to work on an offshore oil rig if they so desire. But this reality took hold only after centuries of struggle and a whole lot of attitude from some very powerful women. Canada can boast a long list of feisty women who fought to be the first in their field, demanded equality, demanded the right to vote and corrected misguided definitions that said women weren't "persons" under the law. It's because of these courageous women, many of whom are quoted below, that we can hold our heads high and say, "I'm nobody's baby."

COPPS: Is there a doctor in the House?
CROSBIE: Just quieten down, baby. You bunch of poltroons can shout all you like. The Rat Pack can quieten down. The titmice can quieten down.
COPPS: I am 32 years old, I am elected Member of Parliament from Hamilton East, and I'm nobody's baby.

–Exchange between MP Sheila Copps and Cabinet Minister John Crosbie in the House of Commons, 1986

Never in any land has the need for intelligent womanhood been so great as in the Dominion of Canada today. And never has the opportunity for woman's service been as wide and glorious.

–Charlotte Whitton (1896–1975), mayor of Ottawa

I believe that never was a country better adapted to produce a great race of women than this Canada of ours, nor a race of women better adapted to make a great country.

–Emily Murphy (1868–1933), Alberta judge, social activist and writer

Whatever my sex, I'm no lady.

–Charlotte Whitton (1896–1975), mayor of Ottawa

There are still more areas to be conquered and more battles to be won...

–Muriel McQueen Fergusson (1899–1997), senator

Most men seem bound by some silent compact that women must never again walk alone in the gardens of opportunity, or be suffered to enjoy equal access to the fruits of knowledge or power.

–Charlotte Whitton (1896–1975), mayor of Ottawa

I believe women suffrage would be a retrograde movement, that it would break up the home, and that it would throw the children into the arms of the servant girls.

–Sir Rodmond Roblin (1853–1937), politician

There are two categories of women. Those who are women and those who are men's wives.

–Charlotte Whitton (1896–1975), mayor of Ottawa

After I realized how you people live, I didn't want the things I had before. I left everything because I wanted to show you I love you people and want to help you.

–Anna Mae Aquash (1945–75),
Native spokesperson, explaining why she was helping
women on the Pine Ridge Reservation

Whatever she does woman must do twice as well as any man to be thought of just half as good...luckily it's not difficult.

–Charlotte Whitton (1896–1975), mayor of Ottawa

What I wanted was not shelter and safety, but liberty and opportunity.

–Martha Black, OBE (also known as the First Lady of the Yukon) (1866–1957), Yukon pioneer, naturalist and MP

I think also it is a duty I owe to my profession and to my sex to show that a woman has the right to the practice of her profession and cannot be condemned to abandon it merely because she marries. I cannot conceive how women's colleges, inviting and encouraging women to enter professions can be justly founded or maintained denying such a principle.

–Harriet Brook (1876–1933), nuclear physicist

The true liberation of women cannot take place without the liberation of men. Basically the women's liberation movement is not only feminist in inspiration, it is also humanist. Let men and women look at one another honestly and try together to give society a new set of values.

–Therese Casgrain (1896–1981), politician and activist

Speak up gentlemen; I'm not opposed to male participation in government.

–Charlotte Whitton (1896–1975), mayor of Ottawa, at a council meeting in 1960

Old maids are the wise virgins of this earth. The married women took the terrible men they refused.

–Kit Coleman (1864–1915), pioneer journalist

The purpose of woman's life is just the same as the purpose of man's life—that she may make the best possible contribution to the generation in which she is living.

–Louise McKinney (1868–1931), Alberta MLA and social activist

I bethought me this evening that the moments were few ere 1880 became for all time a part of history not the least interesting part to me being the fact that our Queen's college opened its doors to Women. I regret very much that so few appear to avail themselves of the grand opportunity.

–Dr. Jenny Gowanlock Trout (1841–1921), medical doctor

Although my sex does not permit me to have inclinations other than those it demands of me, allow me nevertheless, Madame, to tell you that, like many men, I have feelings which incline me to glory.

–Madeleine de Vercheres (1687–1747),
who took command of Fort de Vercheres at the age of 14 and
defended it against attacking Iroquois

Although it was against the rules to stunt with a passenger, on my first lesson he did spins, loops and zooms thinking he could either frighten me or find out how much courage I possessed! I loved it and showed up for my next lesson.

–Eileen Vollick (1908–68), Canada's first female pilot

Well, my philosophy has always been that until all of us have made it, none of us had made it.

–Rosemary Brown (1930–2003), politician and feminist

Woman is the ultimate. Mother Earth belongs to woman, not man. She carries the void.

–Agnes Whistling Elk, female Manitoba shaman, in 1986

Women have no surnames of their own. Their names are literally sirnames. Women only have one name that is ours, our first or given name.

–Margaret Laurence (1926–87), writer

No woman can become or remain degraded without all women suffering.

–Emily Murphy (1868–1933), Alberta judge, social activist and writer

I do not want to be the angel of any home; I want for myself what I want for other women, absolute equality. After that is secured, then men and women can take turns at being angels.

–Agnes Macphail (1890–1954), first woman MP in Canada

We have taught the world that "woman power" is about the cheapest power on earth. We never put a value on the labour which goes into this or that task.

–Violet McNaughton (1879–1968), journalist and first president of the Women Grain Growers of Saskatchewan

I remember my first solo (in the CF-18 Hornet). There I was taxiing out to the end of the runway thinking to myself, "Can you imagine this, look at me driving this $35 million jet!"

–Major Deanna Brasseur (1953–), one of the first two women in the world trained to fly jet fighters in combat

Does feminist mean a large unpleasant person who'll shout at you or someone who believes women are human beings. To me it's the latter, so I sign up.

–Margaret Atwood (1939–), author

In its 1992 annual update of women's status, the National Action Committee alerted women to a bleak future: about 75 percent of (Canadian) females live out the last quarter of their lives in poverty.

–Marlene Webber (1947–), writer

Behind every great man is a woman rolling her eyes.

–Jim Carrey (1962–), actor

Every woman is wrong until she cries, and then she is right, instantly.

–Thomas C. Haliburton (1796–1865), writer

What I've always resented about Women's Lib is that it always told me we were equal—when I always knew women were superior. I prefer being a woman to anything else.

–Barbara Amiel (1940–), columnist

Any woman who tells the truth about herself is a feminist.

–Alice Munro (1931–), writer

Woman has had, from creation, distinctly defined duties, and until the power of education and influence is brought to bear upon these duties, and she has demonstrated her ability to do her own work well, she has no right to infringe on man's prerogative.

–Adelaide Hoodless, founder of the Women's Institute, in 1902

Woman's place in the new order is to bring imagination to work on life's problems. Without vision, which is another word for imagination—the people perish. It is vision that is needed now, rather than logic, and we have a right to expect it from women with their tender hearts and quick sympathies. We look to them to save the situation. The hand that rocks the cradle will surely never rock the boat!

–Nellie McClung (1873–1951), writer, activist and Alberta MLA

If members of my sex appear at times to be inadequate, it must be because a wise God created them to match the men.

–E. Cora Hind (1861–1942), agricultural specialist

Women are like Canadians 10 years ago: timid, self-contemptuous, overlooked. It is no accident that the struggle for women's liberation and the growth of Canadian nationalism are flourishing together.

–Myrna Kostash, writer, in 1974

Men who are attractive to most women are rarities, in this country, at any rate. I think that it is because a man, to be attractive, must be free to give his whole time to it, and the Canadian male is so hounded by taxes and the rigors of our climate that he is lucky to be alive, without being irresistible as well.

–Robertson Davies (1913–95), author

WELCOME TO OUR WORLD

Canada wasn't always welcoming to its newcomers. The first settlers to this huge geography thought they were upholding their responsibilities by taming the land the way they knew best. There was little understanding of the First Nations' way of life and minimal acceptance for ethnic customs different from their own. Through a gradual appreciation for cultural diversity, our country has developed into the great Northern mosaic.

A DIFFICULT JOURNEY

This is an English-speaking province and it is the duty of the government to see that every pupil of the public schools is given a sufficient education in English to equip him, in part at least, for the business of life...We must Canadianize this generation of foreign-born settlers, or this will cease to be a Canadian country in any real sense of the term.

–John W. Dafoe (1866–1944), journalist and liberal reformer

What does the ordinary Canadian know about our immigrants? He classifies all men as white men and foreigners. The foreigners he thinks of as the men who dig the sewers and get into trouble at the police court. They are all supposed to dress in outlandish garb, to speak a barbarian tongue, and to smell abominably.

–J.S. Woodsworth (1874–1942), writer and social activist

Having suffered ostracism and condescension because of their foreignness, it seemed as though all the national energy of the people had been expended to acquire a blameless Canadian skin, Canadian habits, and Canadian homes.

–Laura Salverson (1890–1970), writer

No Chinaman, Japanese, or Indian shall have his name placed on the Register of Voters for any Electoral District, or be entitled to vote at any election.

–British Columbia Provincial Elections Act, 1901

We weren't the enemy. Neither were we alien. But we lost everything.

–Hide Hyodo Shimizu (1908–99), Japanese immigrant

The story of the Japanese in Canada tells us something about universal corruption, universal greed, universal ignorance, blindness, and fear. We are as one with other countries of the world, dancing the same dance in our stained underwear.

–Joy Kogawa (1935–), writer

Immigration is a privilege, which we have a perfect right to grant or deny as we see fit, and when an alien applies for permission to come to Canada, he is like someone applying for membership in a club.

–J.W. Pickersgill (1905–97), in 1955 when serving as Minister of Immigration

Multiculturalism, really, is folklore. It is a "red herring." The notion was devised to obscure "the Québec business," to give an impression that we are all ethnics and do not have to worry about special status for Québec.

–René Lévesque (1922–87), Québec premier

The proper and natural place to have one's roots is where a tree has them: underground.

–George Jonas (1935–), writer

There are presumably expatriate Jews available but we would wish to be very sure of the personality and ability of a candidate. These matters are easier to arrange in the University when there is not too high a proportion of Jewish blood.

–Charles H. Best (1899–1978),
co-discovered insulin, in a letter dated February 24, 1939

What the hell does multiculturalism mean? We can't even get our own culture going; what are they talking about? How can it be "multi" when there isn't even one? I mean it's all wild. It's beautiful on paper, but its meaning is blank.

–Scott Symons (1933–), writer and cultural commentator

Maintaining my roots is my business, not the government's. If I want my child to speak the ancestral language I'll see to it that he does. It is my affair, not the Canadian taxpayer's.

–George Jonas (1935–), writer

I know what multiculturalism means. It means the Scots own the banks and the Portuguese get to clean them.

–Herb Denton, correspondent,
in *The Globe and Mail* on October 30, 1990

We peer so suspiciously at each other that we cannot see that we Canadians are standing on the mountaintop of human wealth, freedom and privilege.

–Pierre Elliott Trudeau (1919–2000), prime minister

A GRADUAL UNDERSTANDING

Growing pains, assessed and analyzed, can result in strength of character, a change in perspective and sometimes a new way of thinking.

Strong men were misunderstood, maligned; timid women hesitated on the threshold of public life. But they all heard the whispering of the Great Spirit: "There is room for your thinkers, your men of vision, your lovers of freedom. Come, and I will make of you a great nation."

–Mabel Dunham (1881–1957), writer and librarian

To coloured women we have a word—we have broken the "Editorial Ice" whether willingly or not for your class in America, so go to editing as many of you are willing and able and as soon as you may, if you think you are ready.

–Mary Ann Shadd (Cary) (1823–93),
pioneer journalist, editor and publisher

We have never been a melting pot. The fact is we are more like a tossed salad. We are green, some of us are oily, and there's a little vinegar injected when you get up to Ottawa.

–Arnold Edinborough (1767–1849),
British writer and cultural commentator

Tolerant is a slightly negative word. It's like saying, "You smell, but I can hold my breath."

–David Lam (1923–), lieutenant-governor of BC

Canada is where diversity comes together.

–Joe Clark (1939–), prime minister

Nearly half a century ago, in the crisis of wartime, the Government of Canada wrongfully incarcerated, seized the property, and disenfranchised thousands of citizens of Japanese ancestry. We cannot change the past. But we must, as a nation, have the courage to face up to these historical facts.

–Brian Mulroney (1939–), prime minister

Too many people in Canada forget that people crawl across minefields to get here.

–Ignat Kaneff (1926–), Bulgarian-born developer,
recorded by Pat Brennan in *The Toronto Star*, February 6, 1989

We have forgotten that one cannot forge a nation by encouraging separateness under the rubric of multiculturalism. A person's roots are a private matter, not a subject of public subsidy.

–Barbara Amiel (1940–), columnist

We must come to the point where we realize the concept of race is a false one. There is only one race, the human race.

–Dan Aykroyd (1952–), actor, writer, producer and film director

I hope that people will finally come to realize that there is only one "race"—the human race—and that we are all members of it.

–Margaret Atwood (1939–), writer

Curiosity is part of the cement that holds society together.

–Robertson Davies (1913–95), writer

Canada has created harmony and co-operation among ethnic groups, and it must take this experience to the world because there is yet to be such an example of harmony and co-operation among ethnic groups.

–Valentyn Moroz (1936–), Ukrainian dissident and immigrant

I think Canada, more than most countries, is a place you choose to live in. It's easy for us to leave, and many of us have.

–Margaret Atwood (1939–), writer

A D.P. is not a Displaced Person; a D.P. is a Delayed Pioneer!

–Jan Rubes (1920–), Czech-born singer and actor

It no longer matters who were the first Canadians or who were the second Canadians. There is no race and there are no prizes for being the 32nd kind of Canadian and there is no stigma in being the 77th kind of Canadian. There is only one sorrow and one pity we must avoid at all costs—let none of us be the last Canadians.

–David Crombie (1936–), in 1977 when serving as mayor of Toronto

The post-1945 migration (which unlike earlier such movements consisted mainly of people who have stayed in Canada) has been one of the most potent factors in preserving our culture and our way of life from absorption into the general North America pattern.

–George Woodcock (1912–95), writer

The right to live in Canada, with all its injustices, is so great a privilege that countless millions of the world's desperate people would come here tomorrow if they could.

–Bruce Hutchison (1901–92), newspaper editor and author

I got the biggest thrill in some of these small places out west. The halls would be filled with people, and sitting there in the front would be the first Ukrainian immigrants with shawls and hands gnarled from work. I would speak for about 20 minutes in English, then I would switch to Ukrainian and the tears would run down their faces. A man came to me one day and he said, "Now I can die, I have met a minister of Ukrainian extraction."

–Michael Starr (1910–2000), MP, in 1958

No one is a Canadian any more. We are all Ukrainian-Canadians or Italian-Canadians or Albertan-Canadians or Québec-Canadians.

–Laura Sabia (1916–96), feminist spokesperson, in 1979

Our great advantage, over other nations, is our tradition of diversity, which was born of the historic necessity of English- and French-speaking Canadians working together and which has blossomed into a basic respect for the multitude of cultures, which make up Canada.

–Joe Clark (1939–), prime minister, in 1976

It's spelt H-N-A-T-Y-S-H-Y-N, and it looks like the first line of an eye chart.

–Ramon Hnatyshyn (1934–2002), MP,
spelling his Ukrainian surname in 1976

EARNING YOUR KEEP

What's intriguing about Canada is the variety of work available. You can aspire to traditional roles such as doctor, lawyer or politician. Or you might instead choose to run a logging truck, grow fruit in the Okanagan or operate a trapline. From sea to sea, the North Pole to our southernmost latitudes, the variety of jobs available is limited only by our imagination.

THE WORLD OF WORK

To work at something that's challenging and rewarding is often as much a need as eating and breathing. Just ask your retired neighbour. Chances are he'll tell you he's busier now than he's ever been—and he's not even getting paid!

Every person and every class of persons shall enjoy the right to obtain and retain employment without discrimination with respect to the compensation, terms, conditions or privileges of employment because of the race, creed, religion, colour or ethnic or national origin of such person or class of persons.

–Saskatchewan Bill of Rights Act, 1947

And I say to you that if you bring curiosity to your work it will cease to be merely a job and become a door through which you enter the best that life has to give you.

–Robertson Davies (1913–95), writer

If Canada became a country where reasonable profits could be made safely and honestly, industry and enterprise would flourish and tax revenues would increase as unemployment declined.

–Peter Worthington, journalist, in 1987

The seed of our toil watered with the sweat of our brows, has now ripened into the fruits of our labours.

–Lionel Forsyth, chancellor of University of King's College (Halifax), addressing a group of DOSCO employees in 1957

If they don't have a shovel, they should get one, because otherwise we're going to give them one. If anybody is able to work but refuses to pick up the shovel, then we will find ways and means of dealing with that person.

–William Vander Zalm (1934–),
in 1975 when serving as BC Minister of Human Resources

In Canada preserving energy and industry, with sobriety, will overcome all obstacles, and in time will place the very poorest family in a position of substantial comfort that no personal exertions alone could have procured for them elsewhere.

–Catharine Parr Traill (1802–99), Ontario pioneer and writer

AND LACK OF WORK

For those Canadians who lived through the Great Depression, counting pennies became second nature. There were not enough jobs, and Prairie families who relied on their gardens for their food were left hungry as the Prairies became a grasshopper-infested dust bowl. Throughout history, natural disaster has not been the only thing preventing abundance for all. The working poor have always been a large part of our population, often because someone else has gotten rich from their efforts.

So long as Canadian economic activity is dominated by the corporate elite, and so long as workers' rights are confined within their present limits, corporate requirements for profit will continue to take precedence over human needs.

From *The Waffle Manifesto: For an Independent Socialist Canada*, 1969

The bubble burst, the companies toppled, Canada, a country built on compromise, compromised again. We ended up with two roads—one too many—a private road that made money, a public road saddled with debt for which the taxpayers, not the bondholders, were charged. It's unnerving to realize that in the seven worst years of the Depression, Ottawa shovelled out more money to service the debt of the CNR than it did in relief payments to the dispossessed.

Pierre Berton (1920–2004), author

Land of Bull and Bailing-Wire.

–This phrase used to describe Canada during the Great Depression, referring to politicians who spoke of the need to "make do"

Every newspaper except their own was suppressed; water pressure was reduced to thirty pounds, for that is enough to bring it to one storey buildings, and the *Western Labour News* stated that it is in one storey buildings that the "workers" live, the inference being that it did not matter whether the other people lived or not...There was something so despotic and arrogant about all this, that even indifferent citizens rallied to the call for help.

–Nellie McClung (1873–1951), writer, activist and Alberta MLA

POVERTY AND GREED

Poverty is an unnecessary affliction that begins in the womb and can be solved with a quart of milk a day.

–Agnes Higgins (1911–1985), nutritionist, in 1973

Poverty isn't being broke; poverty is never having enough.

–Betty Jane Wylie (1931–) and Lynne MacFarlane, writers, from their co-authored *Everywoman's Money Book* (1989)

To be poor is to feel apathy; alienation from society, entrapment, and hopelessness and to believe that whatever you do will not turn out successfully.

–*Report of the Canadian Royal Commission on the Status of Woman*, 1970

Headlines pass; breadlines continue.

–Robin Skelton (1925–), writer

Poverty in Canada is real.... Its persistence, at a time when the bulk of Canadians enjoy one of the highest standards of living in the world, is a disgrace.

–From the *Fifth Annual Review* of the Economic Council of Canada, dated 1968

You can never have international peace as long as you have national poverty.

–Stephen Leacock (1869–1944), humorist and writer

Too many men salt away money in the brine of other people's tears.

–"Eye-Opener Bob" Edwards (1864–1922), pioneer journalist

LIFE AND THE ART OF LIVING

Most often, life is something of a roller coaster ride. There are highs and lows, dips and turns, and some days leave you feeling better than others. Of course, everyone has their own definition for the meaning of life—and their own views of what makes life a joy to live or a living hell.

REFLECTIONS THROUGH THE AGES

By the time we hit 50, we have learned our hardest lessons. We have found out that only a few things are really important. We have learned to take life seriously, but never ourselves.

–Marie Dressler (1869–1934), Canadian-born actress

People who take everything seriously live in a kind of hell. Everything tortures them.

–Margaret Atwood (1939–), writer

I am confused, therefore I am.

–Jack Ludwig, writer, in 1960

Life's an awfully lonesome affair. You come into the world alone and you go out of the world alone yet it seems to me you are more alone while living than even going and coming.

–Emily Carr (1871–1945), artist and writer

Those who can soar to the highest heights can also plunge to the deepest depths, and the natures which enjoy most keenly are those which also suffer most sharply.

–Lucy Maud Montgomery (1874–1942), writer

You cannot be better than the moment in time in which you find yourself.

–Vivian Rakoff, professor of psychiatry at the University of Toronto

Once you commit yourself to "what if," anything is possible.

–Betty Jane Wylie (1931–), writer

This is the paradox about life—that every individual is different. But together we're all alike.

–Yvon Deschamps (1935–), comedian

There's a terrible yearning in all of us for life to somehow go on. The only way to deal with it is to think of every day as dying. Each of those days you live as fully as possible within that day. So that when you come to die, you haven't half-lived.

–Elizabeth Kilbourn, Anglican priest, in 1979

From great-grandparents to great-grandchildren we are only knots in a string.

–Naskapi Indian proverb

Maannamit

–An Inuktitut proverbial expression meaning, "From now on, it is in the future."

I really feel like life will dictate itself. You should allow it to unfold as naturally as possible. Just go with the flow. When you're really desperate, you say a few prayers and hope for the best. That's the way I've always lived my life.

–Shania Twain (1965–), singer

Life is a horror movie, starring people you know.

–Richard J. Needham (1912–96), columnist

We seldom or never learn, until too late, to distinguish which act or word, apparently trifling, is big with consequences we should shrink from—could we only see them.

–Francis W. Grey, writer, in 1899

I had the stubborn and stupid conviction that I ought to find the magical in real life.

–Morley Callaghan (1903–90), writer

I've had a really good career, but quite frankly I'd rather be a well-rounded human being than a well-rounded performer.

–Anne Murray (1945–), singer

CHARACTER

Strength, steadfastness, determination, confidence—a person's character is built of this and so much more.

I may be wrong, but I'm never in doubt.

–Marshall McLuhan (1911–80), educator and media philosopher

It's the moment you think you can't that you realize you can.

–Celine Dion (1968–), singer

The real test of character is in surprise. It is the unforeseen crisis, the sudden calamity, the unexpected shock, when the man is off guard, which shows truly what he is.

–Archibald MacMechan (1862–1933), writer

That's what makes a man great; his flashes of insight, when he pierces through the nonsense of his time, and gets at something that really matters.

–Robertson Davies (1913–95), writer

Never retract, never explain, never apologize—get the thing done and let them howl.

–Nellie McClung (1873–1951), writer, activist and Alberta MLA

A slave is...a man who waits for someone else to come and free him.

–Anastasia M. Shkilnyk, writer, in 1985

Never run from anything...till you've had a good look at it. Most times it's not worth running from.

Thomas H. Raddall (1903–94), writer

There is only one way in the world to be distinguished: Follow your instinct! Be yourself, and you'll be somebody. Be one more blind follower of the blind; and you will have the oblivion you desire.

–Bliss Carman (1861–1929), poet

There is no resignation in Nature, no quiet folding of the hands, no hypocritical saying, "Thy will be done!" and giving in without a struggle. Resignation is a cheap and indolent human virtue, which has served as an excuse for much spiritual slothfulness. It is still highly revered and commended. It is so much easier to sit down and be resigned than to rise up and be indignant.

–Nellie McClung (1873–1951), writer, activist and Alberta MLA

Do not be discouraged by lack of immediate success. Bernard Shaw flowered at 17 but nobody smelled him until he was 40.

Robertson Davies (1913–95), writer

If you want work well done, select a busy man—the other kind has no time.

–"Eye-Opener Bob" Edwards (1864–1922), pioneer journalist

To know the universe is to know yourself. To know yourself is to journey to the end of the universe.

–T.B. Pawlicki, writer and theorist, in 1984

It only seems as if you're doing something when you worry.

–Lucy Maud Montgomery (1874–1942), writer

Great obstacles make great leaders.

–Billy Diamond (1949–), Cree leader

People can earn a living by accident; but learning to live is an art.

–Earl Work, motivational speaker, in 1989

A ship in the harbour is safe, but that is not what ships are built for.

–Punch Imlach (1918–87), hockey coach

The best preparation for tomorrow is to do today's work superbly well.

–William Osler (1849–1919), physician

It's important to give it all you have while you have the chance.

–Shania Twain (1965–), singer

You will find as you look back upon your life that the moments when you have really lived are the moments when you have done things in the spirit of love.

–Henry Drummond (1851–97), poet

A man is only as good as what he loves.

–Saul Bellow (1915–2005), writer

Only a fool expects to be happy all the time.

–Robertson Davies (1913–95), writer

Time past and time future are both present in time present. We flesh out what we are with what we were; the better to be what we will be.

–Donald Sutherland (1935–), actor

Courage and cheerfulness will not only carry you over the rough places in life, but will enable you to bring comfort and help to the weak-hearted and will console you in the sad hours.

–William Osler (1849–1919), physician

FRIEND OR FOE?

Sometimes it's tough to know who your friends are. Sometimes human unpredictability results in disappointments from our friends and a drawing of strength from our foe. Then again, the truly jaded simply prefer to keep their own company.

Since I no longer expect anything from mankind, except madness, meanness, and mendacity; egotism, cowardice, and self-delusion, I have stopped being a misanthrope.

–Irving Layton (1912–2006), poet

Our enemies toughen us up by attacking us; it is our friends who gently sap away our strength.

–Richard J. Needham (1912–96), columnist

It's so easy to be wicked without knowing it, isn't it?

–Lucy Maud Montgomery (1874–1942), writer

Amidst all the sound and fury, I don't expect right to prevail; I don't expect wrong to prevail either; I just expect the sound and fury to prevail.

–Richard J. Needham (1912–96), columnist

The people who influence you are the people who believe in you.

–Henry Drummond (1851–97), poet

The friendship of the selfish is a warm wind from the South when the skies are clear, but when trouble comes it's as cold as the blast of Death.

–George V. Hobart (1867–1926), writer and director

What do these enemies of the human race look like? Do they wear on their foreheads a sign so that they may be told, shunned and condemned as criminals? No. On the contrary, they are the respectable ones. They are honoured. They call themselves, and are called, gentlemen. What a travesty on the name Gentlemen!

–Dr. Norman Bethune (1890–1939), physician

You can always depend upon the enmity of your enemies, but there are times when you cannot depend upon the friendship of your friends.

–"Eye-Opener Bob" Edwards (1864–1922), pioneer journalist

Was there ever a friendship between two women that did not mean a plot against a third?

–Kit Coleman (1864–1915), pioneer journalist

Whether people are good or bad, useful or harmful, depends not on their moral principles or even their conscious aims, but on the strength of their imagination.

–Stephen Vizinczey (1933–), writer

HAPPINESS IS...

...different things to different people—or so the song goes. Judging by the following quotes, it's a saying worthy of merit.

I wish people could achieve what they think would bring them happiness in order for them to realize that that's not really what happiness is.

–Alanis Morisette (1974–), singer-songwriter

Yes, there is tragedy and unhappiness in this life, but there is also happiness and triumph and joy, and on balance, I think life is a joyful thing.

–Knowlton Nash (1927–), TV anchor

I'm walking along my little road to nowhere, and my heart is as full of joy as if I were at the axis of the world.

–Gabrielle Roy (1909–83), writer

There are many different happinesses—and we never have them all at once—because that would be perfect happiness and that is something the gods do not allow to mortals. We have some at one period of our lives and yet others at another. Perfect happiness I have never had—never will have. Yet there have been, after all, many wonderful and exquisite hours in my life.

–Lucy Maud Montgomery (1874–1942), writer

Crying in times of loss is healing. But I try to stop as soon as possible, so I have the strength to face the happiness I suspect is lurking around the corner.

–Lynne Gordon, broadcaster and writer, in 1986

Men and women suffer equally. The tragedy is not that they suffer, but that they suffer alone.

–Sinclair Ross (1908–96), writer

Happiness has been described as the cessation of pain. But if we realize that pain is part of the human condition and unavoidable, we can let go of pain to be happy. Then we can shout from the rooftops knowing that the gods will not punish us for this unseemly outburst.

–Lynne Gordon, broadcaster and writer, in 1984

Happiness equals reality over expectations.

–Dave Nichol, president of Loblaws, in 1984

I'll tell you something. Happiness comes only through real friends. We all have lots of friends but I'm talking about the select few we can go to in troubled times and relax in their company. Beginning with the prime requisite, a good wife, no man can handle more than six. In that respect I have been most fortunate.

–E.P. Taylor (1901–89), capitalist

Whenever I feel anxious, terrified that something will go wrong, I usually search for the cause of my fears. Sometimes I realize that nothing is wrong, all is right, and what I'm afraid of is happiness.

–Lynne Gordon, broadcaster and writer, in 1986

FACING LIFE'S CHALLENGES

Everyone is faced with challenges at some point in their lives. But for some of us, substantial demands are part of daily living. Getting ready for work, driving the car, picking up groceries...the things most of us do in the normal course of a day requires extra planning and focus for people with disabilities. Nothing is taken for granted. At the same time, there is joy with each accomplishment, a quiet nobility that transcends each difficulty and embraces it with strength of character only someone who's been tried and tested can demonstrate.

You have to be the best you can be with what you have.

–Rick Hansen (1958–),
wheelchair athlete and founder of Man in Motion World Tour

He made his too-short life into a marathon of courage and hope.

–Inscription on the tombstone of Terry Fox in the municipal cemetery, Port Coquitlam, BC

People accept your disability if you accept it.

–Harold Russell (1914–2002), amputee spokesperson and actor

My disability is that I cannot use my legs. My handicap is your negative perception of that disability, and thus of me.

–Rick Hansen (1958–),
wheelchair athlete and founder of Man in Motion World Tour

No one knows better than a blind person the value of sight.

–Colonel E.A. Baker (1893–1968), long-time managing director of the Canadian National Institute for the Blind

Life is the development of what you have, with an acceptance of the things you can not change.

–Hugh MacMillan,
director of the Ontario Crippled Children's Centre, in 1989

Keep in mind, though, this eternal truth: Difficulties do not crush men, they make them.

–Arthur Meighen (1874–1960), prime minister, in 1942

It is not what you have lost, but what you have left.

–Harold Russell (1914–2002), amputee spokesperson and actor

There is a mystery in the secret strength of those whose bodies are broken, who seem to do nothing all day, but who remain in the presence of God. Their immobility obliges them to keep their minds and hearts fixed on the essential, on the source of life itself.

–Jean Vanier (1928–), founder of L'Arche,
an international organization that creates communities
for people with developmental disabilities

The label "learning disabled" is not understood by people with several degrees behind their names. This leads to misunderstandings that I may be of considerably lower intelligence than what I truly am. This means that they are prejudiced or in a biased frame of mind when my papers are marked, especially when I am forced to write by hand. Students with disabilities do not get an unfair advantage by having accommodations made to the learning environment; it only levels the playing field when done appropriately.

–Michael Schwake, a print-disabled student, in 2000

The true measure of a civilization rests upon how it cares for its vulnerable members.

–Reva Gerstein, psychologist and educator, in 1984

HOPE

To hope is to see the ray of light in the darkest night.
To hope is to believe that whatever comes your way,
there is purpose in the experience. To hope is...

Hope is faith holding out its hands in the dark.

–George Iles (1852–1942), writer

Hope is a pleasant acquaintance, but an unsafe friend.

–T.C. Haliburton (1796–1865), writer

It is difficult to maintain hope in such a world, and yet I believe there must be hope. I want to proclaim my belief in the social gospel, as a Christian, a woman, a writer, a mother and a member of humanity, a sharer in a life that I believe in some way to be informed by the Holy Spirit.

–Margaret Laurence (1926–87), writer

Confidence is armoured, but hope runs naked.

–Robin Skelton (1925–97), poet

In this world you've just got to hope for the best and prepare for the worst and take whatever God sends.

–Lucy Maud Montgomery (1874–1942), writer

Ideals, hope, ambitions tumble into ruins before the necessity of gaining daily bread.

–Kit Coleman (1864–1915), pioneer journalist

Memory is a form of hope.

–Timothy Findley (1930–2002), writer

IDEAS

Ideas are the building blocks of a nation,
the seed that begets possibility, the means to an answer,
the catalyst without which we become stagnant.

As a rule, the most dangerous ideas are not the ones that divide people, but those on which they agree.

–Stephen Vizinczey (1933–), writer

Neoideophobia (a word of my coinage meaning "fear of new ideas") affects humans worldwide.

–Ian Stevenson, psychiatrist, psychical researcher and author of *Children Who Remember Previous Lives: A Question of Reincarnation* (1987)

Faced with the choice between changing one's mind and proving that there is no need to do so, almost everyone gets busy on the proof.

–J. K. Galbraith (1908–), Canadian/American economist

I believe that to change people's minds—and governments are people—we must not rely solely on economic or other arguments, but must create a sense of imagination.

–M.T. (Terry) Kelly (1946–), writer

You just jot down ideas as they occur to you. The jotting is simplicity itself—it is the occurring that is difficult.

–Stephen Leacock (1869–1944), humorist and writer

Ideas are contagious and epidemic. They break out unexpectedly and without warning. Thought without expression is dynamic and gathers volume by repression. Evolution, when blocked and suppressed, becomes revolution.

–Nellie McClung (1873–1951), writer, activist and Alberta MLA

SELF-IMPROVEMENT

It is all about learning from life.

I acted on the information I have been accumulating since I was three years old.

–Pierre Elliott Trudeau (1919–2000), prime minister

Learning would be exceedingly laborious, not to mention hazardous, if people had to rely solely on the effects of their own actions to inform them what to do. Fortunately, most human behaviour is learned observationally through modelling: from "observi."

–Albert Bandura (1925–), psychologist

An illiterate fool can be a useful fool, he can wash floors, but a fool with a doctorate is deadly. No amount of learning can cure stupidity and higher education positively fortifies it.

–Stephen Vizinczey (1933–), writer

A little learning is a dangerous thing, but a lot of ignorance is just as bad.

–"Eye-Opener Bob" Edwards (1864–1922), pioneer journalist

You have to drop out of school now and then if you want to get an education.

–Pamela Peck, Ph.D.,
cultural anthropologist and author of *The Cannibal's Cookbook*

The faith I cling to, a stubborn but I hope not merely romantic faith in the enduring power of man himself to improve himself—man who, so long as he remains alive, may remake, any moment, his whole future; or even if that future must have an end in our sun's explosion or its dimming, has a present that can be glorious.

–Earle Birney (1904–95), poet

Nearly all knowledge in the world has been acquired at the expense of somebody's burnt fingers.

–"Eye-Opener Bob" Edwards (1864–1922), pioneer journalist

LOVE AND CONFLICT BETWEEN THE GENDERS

In the end, everyone thinks they have a point to make.

The world has suffered long from too much masculinity and not enough humanity.

–Nellie McClung (1873–1951), writer, activist and Alberta MLA

The woman who had never slapped a man across the face was either a whore or ugly.

–Jean-Marie Poupart (1946–2004), writer

In the war between the sexes, we're all volunteers.

–M.T. (Terry) Kelly, writer, in the *Globe and Mail* on June 23, 1979

It defeats me to spend a good evening's conversation only to find that the man in question considered the exchange of thoughts a kind of mandatory preamble to be tolerated in order to get laid. It doesn't make sense.

–Charlotte Vale Allen (1941–), writer

In point of intellect, the average woman cannot reason and think. But she can argue.

–Stephen Leacock (1869–1944), humorist and writer

If a man understands one woman he should let it go at that.

–"Eye-Opener Bob" Edwards (1864–1922), pioneer journalist

As Goethe said, it is the Eternal Feminine that beckons us ever onward. He did not mention the Eternal Old Woman who holds us back.

–Robertson Davies (1913–95), writer

Women know men better than they know themselves and better than men ever suspect.

–Sir John Willison (1856–1927), journalist

Just about any man and woman can share a bedroom, but sharing a bathroom—ah, that is something else again.

–Richard J. Needham (1912–96), humour columnist

The bitter truth about women is that their minds work precisely like those of men: the bitter truth about men is they are too vain to admit it.

–Robertson Davies (1913–95), writer

OUR HEROES

Although we don't typically boast about the great things Canada has produced, we do have our heroes. We just don't talk about them very much. We do, however, have strong opinions about heroism.

Then, in Canada, we like our heroes made to order, and in our own image. They mustn't be too good and, above all, not too different.

–David Milne (1882–1953), artist

It is part of the civic genius—part of the Canadian genius, too—to reduce the heroic to the banal.

–Jan Morris (1926–), Welsh travel writer, in 1990

The pattern is clear. Canadians distrust heroes, partly because heroism is always a kind of imposition; the hero is dominating us by his strength, by his brute courage, and we have become suspicious of such qualities...We suspect the sheer gigantic irrationalism of the heroic, for we like to consider ourselves reasonable people.

–George Woodcock (1912–95), writer

What I consider a hero is a guy who goes to work every day and supports his family. The ordinary guy. I think to hold it together nowadays is a heroic enterprise.

–Leonard Cohen (1934–), poet and singer

SUCCESS AND FAILURE

Failure is nothing more than a stepping stone,
and a necessary building block, to success.

If you have made mistakes, there is always another chance for you. You may have a fresh start any moment you choose, for this thing we call "failure" is not the falling down, but the staying down.

–Mary Pickford (1893–1979), Canadian-born Hollywood actress

If I have any advice to pass on, as a successful man, it is this: if one wants to be successful, one must think; one must think until it hurts.

–Roy Thompson (1894–1976), publisher, in 1975

Striving, striving, and more striving—every day, every hour, every moment…I am bold enough to say, though not in the literal sense, that I almost prefer striving without success to success without striving.

–Georges P. Vanier (1888–1967), governor general of Canada, in 1960

A very wise woman, an elderly writer of poems and stories, once said to me, "Success is failure with invisible mending."

–John Herbert (1926–), writer, in 1978

Dare to dream—dare to try—dare to fail—dare to succeed.

–G. Kinsley Ward, entrepreneur, in 1985

WAR AND PEACE

Canadians are known more for their peacekeeping efforts than their offensive tactics. War is simply un-Canadian. We don't like conflict. We don't see the point to war. We'd much rather talk about our problems over a cup of Tim Horton's coffee.

Very little is known about the War of 1812 because the Americans lost it.

–Eric Nicol (1919–), humorist and writer

The politicians, who once stated that war was too complex to be left to the generals, now act as though peace were too complex to be left to themselves.

–Pierre Elliott Trudeau (1919–2000), prime minister

How many dead do you have to see in a war before you know it is Death you are fighting for?

–Raymond Souster (1921–), poet

The idea that every 20 years this country should automatically and as a matter of course take part in a war overseas for democracy or self-determination of other small nations, that a country which has all it can do to run itself should feel called upon to save, periodically, a continent that cannot save itself, and to these ends risk the lives of its people, risk bankruptcy and political disunion, seems to many a nightmare and sheer madness.

–William Lyon Mackenzie King, prime minister, in 1939 during a House of Commons debate

The truth about the war comes out 20 years after you died in it.

–Richard J. Needham (1912–96), columnist

The grim fact is that we prepare for war like precocious giants and for peace like retarded pygmies.

–Lester B. Pearson (1897–1972), prime minister

The Canadian is a withdrawer from involvement...We're the most politically illiterate people in any developed country in the world, and politically we are dull...We go too far with political indifference.

–Charles Lynch, columnist, in 1976

I know that truth is one of the first victims of war.

–J.S. Woodsworth, CCF leader, casting the sole dissenting vote against Canada's declaration of war on Germany, House of Commons, September 8, 1939

There was a valid distinction between an offensive and a defensive weapon; if you were in front of it, it was offensive; if you were behind it, it was defensive.

–Lester B. Pearson (1897–1972), prime minister

There are only two species that actually go to war, man and ants. There is no possibility of any change in the ants.

–John G. Diefenbaker (1895–1979), prime minister, during a debate in the House of Commons

War is what happens when language fails.

–Margaret Atwood (1939–), writer

The only defence is peace.

–Therese Casgrain (1896–1981), politician and activist

I believe in intervention and personal responsibility. In fact, to me, diplomacy is getting what you want without actually going to war.

–Adrienne Clarkson (1939–), governor general of Canada

Most of the wars and afflictions that have come on the world are due to attempts made by incompetent people to be their brothers' keepers.

–Peter McArthur (1866–1924), writer,
in *The Affable Stranger* (1920)

The true measure of the success of our society is the ideal we hold of justice and the effort we make to achieve that idea.

–John Crosbie (1931–), politician

There never has been a war of Canadian origin, nor for a Canadian cause.

–William Arthur Deacon (1890–1977),
writer, in *My Vision of Canada* (1933)

It is sometimes well to allow sleeping dogs to lie. This, I believe is especially true where they happen to be the dogs of war.

–William Lyon Mackenzie King (1874–1950), prime minister

All ignorance is motivated.

–Marshall McLuhan (1911–80), educator and media philosopher

BREAKING NEW GROUND

Early pioneers saw Canada as alternately challenging and breathtaking. For them, this country was an immeasurable expanse that required endless amounts of work to make it habitable. Rugged, cold, mosquito infested, frightening, barren, dangerous and without the slightest indulgence…there was no end to the fear and uncertainty that clouded the mind of Canada's pioneers. But there was joy too. And awe. And a country was formed.

THE FIRST DAYS OF CANADA

Every little dwelling you see has its lot of land and, consequently, its flock of sheep; and, as the children are early taught to spin, and knit, and help dye the yarn, their parents can afford to see them well and comfortably clothed...Many of these very farms you see in so thriving a condition were wild land thirty years ago, nothing but Indian hunting grounds. The industry of men, and many of them poor men, that had not a rood of land in their own country, has effected this change.

–Catharine Parr Traill (1802–99), Ontario pioneer and writer

Lord, have compassion upon me, a poor unfortunate sinner, 3000 miles from my own country, and 75 from anywhere else.

–John Murray in his *Prayer of an Irish Emigrant* (1784)

The Maple-tree...yields a Sap, which has a much pleasanter taste than the best Lemonade or Cherry-water, and makes the wholesomest drink in the World.

–Baron de La Hontan, French traveller, during his travels, 1683–94

'Tis sweet to hear the Indians singing their hymns of a Sunday night; their rich, soft voices rising in the still evening air. I have often listened to this little choir praising the Lord's name in the simplicity and fervour of their hearts, and have felt it was a reproach that these poor half-civilized wanderers should alone be found to gather together to give glory to God in the wilderness.

–Catharine Parr Traill (1802–99), Ontario pioneer and writer

At the beginning of our trip, I had had doubts whether a father should expose his still young child to such hardships and dangers, but from this day on, I was reassured. You were the first white female who had ever gone West any further than Camp Shunda.

–Martin Nordegg, about his 14-year-old daughter Marcella in his memoir, *To The Town that Bears Your Name, A young woman's journey to Nordegg in 1912* (1995). According to *The Sun* (Vancouver), she made a "thrilling trip across the Pipe Stem pass in the Rocky mountains, a route never previously traversed by a white woman."

With staff in hand, at last I had taken my place in that continuous line of pushing humans and straining animals. Before me, behind me, abreast of me almost every man toted a pack of 60 to 80 pounds, in addition to driving dogs and horses harnessed to sleighs and carts, herding pack ponies and the odd cow, while one woman drove an ox-cart.

–Martha Black, OBE (also known as the First Lady of the Yukon) (1866–1957), Yukon pioneer, naturalist and MP

Hell can't be worse than this trail. I'll chance it.

–An unknown gold seeker on the trail from Edmonton to the Yukon in 1897 penned this note just before shooting himself.

There are few women who do not know their privileges and how to use them, yet there are times when the horizon seems restricted, and we seemed to have reached that horizon, and the limit of all endurance…Then we looked into each other's eyes and said: "Why not? We can starve as well as they; the muskeg will be no softer for us than for them; the ground will be no harder to sleep on; the waters no deeper to swim, nor the bath colder if we fall in," so—we planned a trip.

–Mary T.S. Schaffer (1861–1939), pioneer explorer, on her 1911 expedition to Maligne Lake

As to ghosts or spirits they appear totally banished from Canada. This is too matter-of-fact a country for such supernaturals to visit.

–Catharine Parr Traill (1802–99), Ontario pioneer and writer

This I have fully completed the survey of this part of North America from sea to sea, and by almost innumerable astronomical observations have determined the positions of the mountains, lakes, and rivers, and other remarkable places on the northern part of this continent, the maps of all of which have been drawn, and laid down in geographical position, being now the work of 27 years.

–David Thompson (1770–1857), explorer and surveyor

I lived, hermit-like, in the woods, after the renowned example of Robinson Crusoe, passing my time, not unpleasantly, in healthy labour; building my house and cheering my solitude with the agreeable idea of bringing home my wife and little ones—to a home of my own making.

–Major Samuel Strickland (1806–67), pioneer settler

I have accomplished what I resolved to do—it is done. But I would not, if any one was to offer me the universe, go through again the horrors I have undergone in forming this settlement. But do not imagine I repent it; I like my retirement.

–Thomas Talbot, colonist, in July 1837

When the house is completed, we shall have a verandah in front and at the south side…in which we can dine, and have the advantage of cool air, protected from the glare of the sunbeams. The Canadians call these verandahs "stoups." Few houses, log or frame, are without them.

–Catharine Parr Traill (1802–99), Ontario pioneer and writer

"Here Before Christ"

–early 19th century saying used by Northern hunters interpreting the Hudson's Bay Company stores' initials.

Pioneers did not produce original works of art, because they were creating original human environments; they did not imagine utopias because they were shaping them.

–George Woodcock (1912–95), writer

The colonists lived in a world of wood. The pine forest was everywhere on the mainland; only Newfoundland had to make do with stunted trees poking up from the rock.

–Michael Bliss (1941–), historian and writer

The Americans talk, with pride, of being the New World, the cradle of accomplishment. But we Canadians settled the harsher half of the North American continent. It was easier to build Virginia than to build Ontario.

–Joe Clark (1939–), prime minister

CIVILIZING THE CIVILIZED

The establishment of new settlements meant the need to establish law and order in the wilderness.

We have upwards of 100 licensed houses and perhaps as many more which retail spirituous liquors without license; so that the business of one half of the town is to sell rum and the other half to drink it.

–Anonymous, 1760, describing Halifax, NS

It was all very simple; we had to choose between the English of Boston and the English of London. The English of London were farther away and we hated them less.

–Henri Bourassa (1868–1952), politician

You don't enact good laws, you grow them.

–Vincent C. MacDonald, Dean of Law at Dalhousie University, in 1950

The purpose of law is to turn passion to reason.

–F.R. Scott (1899–1985), poet, in the 1970s

Canadian law makes it a crime to "alarm" Her Majesty the Queen.

–Nigel Napier-Andrews, TV producer and writer, from the book *This Is the Law? A Selection of Silly Laws from Around the World* (1976)

TORIES, GRITS AND ASSORTED EXTRAS

There's no doubt our Canadian leaders face challenges in deciding our country's public policy. When our country began, it was tough enough with only the Tories and Grits debating and arguing. In January 2006, there were 15 political parties fighting for seats in the House of Commons. Just imagine the floor of the House should representatives from all 15 parties capture seats! Who'd have thought politics could be so entertaining?

HOW TO BUILD A GREAT CANADA

The great majority of nations have been formed, not by people who desired intensely to live together, but rather by people who could not live separately.

–Jean-Charles Bonenfant, sociologist and author of *L'Esprit de 1867* (1963), by Ramsay Cook in *Canada and the French-Canadian Question* (1966)

You have to give them something they can't get elsewhere. What you've got to give the people is a sense of community, a sense that we have something that's special to this country, that nobody else can understand.

–Pierre Berton (1920–2004), writer

A nation is a body of people who have done great things together in the past and who hope to do great things together in the future.

–F.H. Underhill (1889–1971), historian

Three years ago when in England, I visited one of those models of Gothic architecture, which the hand of genius, guided by an unerring faith, had molded into a harmonious whole. The cathedral was made of granite, oak and marble. It is the image of the nation I wish to see Canada become. For her, I want the granite to remain the granite, the oak to remain the oak, the marble to remain the marble. Out of these elements I would build a nation great among the nations of the world.

–Sir Wilfrid Laurier (1841–1919), prime minister

WHAT CANADIANS SAY ABOUT POLITICS

...their allegiances, their fears, their criticisms, their hopes and their views of Canada.

In Pierre Elliott Trudeau, Canada has at last produced a political leader worthy of assassination.

–Irving Layton (1912–2006), poet

Many Canadian nationalists harbour the bizarre fear that should we ever reject royalty, we would instantly mutate into Americans, as though the Canadian sense of self is so frail and delicate a bud, that the only thing stopping it from being swallowed whole by the U.S. is an English lady in a funny hat.

–Will Ferguson, writer

The shock of knowing how their country is really run would, it is assumed, be too great for Canadians to bear; and they, themselves, avert their eyes.

–Edgar Z. Friedenberg, political scientist, in 1980

Governments are like underwear. They start smelling pretty bad if you don't change them once in a while.

–Margaret (Ma) Murray (1908–82),
pioneer newspaperwoman and publisher

Everybody says Canada is a hard country to govern, but nobody mentions that for some people it's a hard country to live in. Still, if we all run away, it will never be any better.

–Robertson Davies (1913–95), writer

The crisis of Canada today is the combination of economic problems facing us and the increasing impotency of governments that lack either the will or the resources to do much about it. The tragedy of Canada today is that just when we need a country that's pulling together in a common cause, we have one that keeps finding new ways to pull itself apart.

–Angus Reid, entrepreneur and pollster

Most Americans don't understand Canadian political parties. Neither do most Canadians.

–Eric Nicol (1919–), writer and humorist

Politics will eventually be replaced by imagery. The politician will be only too happy to abdicate in favour of his image, because the image will be much more powerful than he could ever be.

–Marshall McLuhan (1911–80), educator and media philosopher

Two weeks before I left Toronto to come to Ottawa in the summer of 1978, a veteran magazine writer took me aside and passed on some worthwhile advice: "The only way to work in Ottawa," he said, and he was speaking from experience, "is to approach each story as if you've just arrived in town that morning, and write each story as if you're leaving town that night."

–Roy MacGregor, journalist, in 1980

One of the toughest things to do when you write about politics is to interest people in what you are writing about, and the Canadian will turn away where the American or European will grab a political topic, form a viewpoint and express it.

–Charles Lynch, columnist, in 1976

Is there a law that prohibits a newspaper photographer from taking a picture of Mulroney with his mouth shut?

–Eleanor Koldofsky (1920–), recording pioneer

Democracy has its faults; the people may run the country to the dogs, but they will run it back again. People, including women, will make mistakes, but in paying for them they will learn wisdom.

–Nellie McClung (1873–1951), writer, activist and Alberta MLA

Canada is probably the world's richest underdeveloped country. We live well by selling our resources to outsiders. We are not primarily a manufacturing country; and until we become one, we will probably remain the world's best-paid colony.

–Alexander Ross, journalist, in 1975

Perhaps, then, Canada is not so much a country as magnificent raw material for a country; and perhaps the question is not "Who are we?" but "What are we going to make of ourselves?"

–Alden Nowlan (1933–83), poet

It simply would not be possible to achieve a consensus across Canada on any one perception of the Canadian identity that could serve as the springboard for Canadian studies.

–T.H.B. Symons, commissioner, in the preface of *To Know Ourselves: The Report of the Commission on Canadian Studies* (1975)

One disadvantage of living in Canada is that one is continually called upon to make statements about the Canadian identity, and Canadian identity is an eminently exhaustible subject.

–Northrop Frye (1912–91), literary philosopher

The deconfederation of Canada began with the unbuilding of the transcontinental railway, a feat of engineering rivaling the Titanic.

–Eric Nicol (1919–), humorist and writer

Somewhere in the cosmos, Machiavelli and Mackenzie King are shaking hands.

–Dalton Camp (1920–2002), columnist

Holy Mackenzie King! It's perfect: the Liberal Gavotte—you take two steps left and two steps right while moving sideways into an uncertain future. And that, my fellow Canadians, is how we got social security without socialism and biculturalism without having to learn French.

–Peter C. Newman (1929–), writer, in 1975

WHAT POLITICIANS SAY ABOUT CANADA

...their fellow politicians, their competing parties and government policy.

Canadians are fed up with a prime minister whose idea of regional development is to give the unemployed a train ticket to Toronto, and then cancel the train.

–Jean Chrétien (1934–), prime minister, in 1990 when bidding for the leadership of the Liberal Party of Canada

There is more to being a Canadian than simply being a resident of one province or a territory.

–Clyde Wells (1937–), Newfoundland premier

The people of Canada want a citizenship that means holding shared values, and not merely a shared passport.

–Jean Chrétien (1934–), prime minister

The definition of a country is people who create something in common that mean something.

–Bob Rae (1948–), Ontario premier

It's significant that I'm the first leader of the New Democratic Party who was born in Canada. Everybody knows where I'm coming from.

–Ed Broadbent (1936–), leader of the federal NDP

As a Liberal insider once put it: "Somebody is going to say some day, 'Will the real Mr. Trudeau please stand up,' and about 58 people will rise."

–George Radwanski, journalist, in 1978

As far as I can judge, not much good can be done without disturbing something or somebody.

–Edward Blake (1833–1912),
politician, during a speech at Aurora, ON, 1874

If you're blind in Canada, chances are you're unemployed. If you're deaf, or physically or mentally disabled in any way, you're likely to be poor, badly housed, unemployed and on your own. If you're black, or a visible minority, chances are you're in a worse job, with lower pay, less recognition, and less opportunity than your white neighbours.

–Bob Rae (1948–), Ontario NDP premier

You won't find me very interesting. I never do anything but work.

–Tommy Douglas (1904–86),
leader of the NDP; Saskatchewan CCF premier

I think that learned counsel is abusing the privilege of being stupid.

–Sir James Lougheed (1854–1925), politician

And if I can be permitted to turn a phrase, I would say that I'm kind of sorry I won't have you to kick around any more.

–Pierre Elliott Trudeau (1919–2000),
prime minister, directed to reporters on his retirement

I have often thought that my whole political life—my whole life as a matter of fact—could be summed up in the words "printer, preacher, politician, premier—or the descent of man."

–Tommy Douglas (1904–86),
leader of the NDP; Saskatchewan CCF premier

The reason you get into politics is because you don't want to be governed by people who are less good than yourself.

–Pierre Elliott Trudeau (1919–2000), prime minister

One of King's more sycophantic backbenchers said to me, "Isn't that wonderful. There is Mr. King making that sign that Churchill has made his. They are together." I replied, "The V has different meanings. For Churchill it means Victory; for King it means Votes."

–John G. Diefenbaker (1895–1979), prime minister, in 1941

In the long run the overwhelming threat to Canada will not come from foreign investments or foreign ideologies, or even—with good fortune—foreign nuclear weapons. It will come instead from the two-thirds of the people of the world who are steadily falling farther and farther behind in their search for a decent standard of living.

–Pierre Elliott Trudeau (1919–2000), prime minister

Journalists may write their worm's-eye views. Prime ministers are presented with the broader vista. Each story undoubtedly has its place in the history of a nation.

–John G. Diefenbaker (1895–1979), prime minister

I must make increasingly clear to the world that prevention of wrong courses of evil and the like means more than all else that man can accomplish.

–William Lyon Mackenzie King (1874–1950), prime minister, in 1944

Politics isn't everything in life. It's damn important to remember that five hundred feet from the Hill no one thinks about politics more than two minutes a day. If that.

–Marc Lalonde, federal cabinet minister, in 1975

The day that Parliament becomes a slot machine into which you drop a slug and out comes legislation, freedom ends.

–John G. Diefenbaker (1895–1979), prime minister

Our strength is that we all reflect where we are from and respect where others come from. My sense of Canada was formed in the open West and has been broadened by a unique opportunity to see this country whole.

–Joe Clark (1939–), prime minister,
when serving as a Conservative leadership candidate in 1976

If you really want to be ignored, make a speech in the Senate.

–John Morrow Godfrey, senator, in 1974

Sometimes, at international conferences, Canada is celebrated for what we are not. We are not a superpower, not an imperial power, not an aggressive nation. But we are a country deeply involved with the rights of minorities.

–Joe Clark (1939–), prime minister

I am convinced that we may develop in Canada a distinctive type of Socialism. I refuse to follow slavishly the British model or the American model or the Russian model. We in Canada will solve our problems along our own lines.

–J.S. Woodsworth (1874–1942), CCF leader, in 1933

Oppositions clean and purify those in office and we in the opposition are in fact the "detergents of democracy."

–John G. Diefenbaker (1895–1979), prime minister, in 1964 when serving as Leader of the Opposition

Our virtue, as a Canadian community, is precisely that there is not one single way of being a Canadian and no uniform way of expressing our identity. Most of us enjoy that freedom from uniformity. It has let some of us become a Maureen Forrester or a Bobby Orr. It has allowed others to raise good families quietly or to pursue other private goals. Political freedom is rare enough in the world, but the kind of social and cultural freedom which is the hallmark of Canada is even less common.

–Joe Clark (1939–), prime minister, in 1977 when he was Conservative leader

Exquisite in appearance, magnificent in design, but it won't fly.

–John G. Diefenbaker (1895–1979), prime minister, describing the Avro Arrow in 1959

HITTING THE ELECTION TRAIL

Promises, promises, promises and more promises. Along with a healthy dose of damnation for opposing parties. Still, no matter how big the media hoopla, voter apathy continues to rise…

It is totally antiquated. It is really a bit of a farce. Most elections mean another dictator for three or four years.

–William Vander Zalm (1934–), BC premier

The more broken heads and bloody noses there is the more election like.

–Sir David W. Smyth, surveyor general, in 1792

They ran a nearly perfect campaign. The only thing they did wrong was lose.

–Warren Armstrong, Conservative Party campaign manager, in 1962

I know an old lady in Toronto who solemnly assured me that her Conservative cow gave two quarts of milk more each day than it had done before the elections.

–Sir John A. Macdonald (1815–1891), prime minister

It must have been something I did.

–Ross Thatcher, Saskatchewan premier,
in 1971 after the defeat of his party.

Jobs, jobs, jobs.

–Brian Mulroney, prime minister,
during the 1984 election campaign

The 4th of September 1984, when I was honoured to lead the Conservative Party to the greatest victory in the history of Canada, I got 50% of the vote, which meant that at the height of my popularity, the greatest ever in Canadian history, electorally, half of the people were opposed to me that very day.

–Brian Mulroney (1939–), prime minister

The greatest thing in the world is to have someone greeting you, the morning after your party has lost an election, "Good morning, Senator."

–Charles Power, a federal cabinet minister and senator, in 1955

Okay, we've won. What do we do now?

–Brian Mulroney (1939–), prime minister

ADVISOR: Do not concede defeat until the Army vote has come in. It is counted last and can swing close seats.
HATFIELD: It would have to be the Chinese Army!

–Richard Hatfield (1931–), premier of New Brunswick, after his defeat in 1987

I'm not going to let Mr. Mulroney destroy a great 120-year-old dream called Canada.

–John Turner (1929–), prime minister, during the 1988 election campaign when he was leader of the Liberal Party

My boy, the only place in this world that you find unanimity is in the graveyard. And even there, I have heard it said, at election time the dead have been known to vote in various ways!

–Maurice Duplessis (1890–1957), Québec premier

Voter apathy is a big problem and it's getting bigger all the time. To make matters worse—nobody gives a s**t.

–Charlie McKenzie, national campaign chairman and concierge of the Parti Rhinoceros, in 1987

The longest and most carefully defended border in the world is between the government of Canada and the governments of each of the provinces. Canadians have a fascination with federal-provincial relations that most other nations reserve for religion or sex.

–Robert G. Evans, economist and health-care specialist, in 1988

POLITICAL FAUX PAS

I bet if they had the chance they'd like to erase that tape!
Take back those words. Re-write the script. But it's too late.
We all make bloopers now and then,
but politicians who do face an unforgiving public!

Now, the only thing that remains unresolved is the resolution of the problem.

–Thomas Wells (1930–2000), Ontario Minister of Education, in 1976

Our Cabinet is always unanimous—except when we disagree.

–Bill Bennett (1932–), BC premier, in 1979

John Lesage is the only person I know who can strut sitting down.

–John G. Diefenbaker (1895–1979), prime minister, mocking the Québec premier

I am not a lawyer. I have many other faults but that is not among them.

–Ed Broadbent (1936–), NDP leader

If I tell a lie, it's only because I think I'm telling the truth.

–Philip A. Gaglardi (1913–95), BC politician

I only ran for mayor because the others were dodos.

–John Sewell (1940–), mayor of Toronto

Look here, my good man, when the election comes why don't you just go away and vote for the party you support. In fact, why don't you just go away?

–C.D. Howe (1886–1960), politician,
to a heckler after a meeting in Morris, MB in 1957

If this thing starts to snowball it will catch fire right across the country.

–Robert Thompson (1914–97), Social Credit politician, in 1974

LORD MAYOR OF LONDON: If I smell your corsage, will you blush?
CHARLOTTE WHITTON, MAYOR OF OTTAWA: If I pull your chain, will you flush?

–This exchange took place in Ottawa in the 1950s.
The English mayor wore a symbolic chain of office around his neck;
the Canadian mayor, a rose pinned to her evening gown.

I'm speaking off the cuff of my head.

–John Kushner (1922–84), Calgary city councillor

We'll cross that bridge when we fall off it.

–Lester B. Pearson (1897–1972), prime minister

I deny the allegation, and I defy the alligators.

–Allan Lamport (1903–99), Toronto mayor

Let's get that in black and writing.

–S. Rebchuck, Winnipeg city councillor, in the 1950s

Well, don't get your dandruff up.

–John Kushner (1922–84), Calgary city councillor

We kind of had the wool pulled out from under us.

–William Vander Zalm (1934–), BC premier

I'm not against abused women. I'm in favour of them 100 percent.

–Doug Mann, Niagara Falls regional councillor, arguing against increased funding for women's shelters, in 1990

It hurts just as much to have a tooth extracted as it does to have it pulled out.

–John G. Diefenbaker (1895–1979), prime minister

You quietly made your points—loud and clear.

–John Kushner (1922–84), Calgary city councillor

When you're talking about me, keep your mouth shut.

–Allan Lamport (1903–99), Toronto mayor

The only thing I want to see on my ministers' desks is their feet!

–Duff Roblin (1917–), Manitoba premier

I am not denying anything I did not say.

–Brian Mulroney (1939–), prime minister

I am as willing to talk about disappointments as about our achievements. The people of Ontario have never been spoiled by perfection in government.

–William Davis (1929–), Ontario premier

Do you think I want a lot of long-haired professors telling me what to do? If I can't run this country, I will get out.

–R.B. Bennett (1870–1947), prime minister, in 1931

The job of a cabinet minister is to tell the civil service what the public won't stand for.

–Duff Roblin (1917–), Manitoba premier

The fact is the statements are perfectly consistent, but more importantly, I don't have all the facts.

–Paul Martin (1938–), prime minister

A proof is a proof. What kind of a proof? It's a proof. A proof is a proof. And when you have a good proof, it's because it's proven.

–Jean Chrétien (1934–), prime minister,
on the U.S. finding no Iraqi weapons of mass destruction

I'm not going to play politics on the floor of the House of Commons.

–John Turner (1929–), prime minister

BATTLE BETWEEN THE RED AND WHITE

During the Crusades, European soldiers were identified with cloth crosses—the British wore white and the French wore red. It's this tradition that is said to have influenced the choice of red and white for the colours of our Canadian flag, signifying a marriage of sorts between the English and the French in the founding of our vast country. As in a marriage, the relationship between the two groups has had its ups and downs.

The die is cast in Canada: there are two ethnic and linguistic groups; each is too strong and too deeply rooted in the past, too firmly bound to a mother culture, to be able to swamp the other. But if the two will collaborate inside of a truly pluralist state, Canada could become a privileged place where the federalist form of government, which is the government of tomorrow's world, will be perfected.

–Pierre Elliott Trudeau (1919–2000), prime minister

I didn't know at first that there were two languages in Canada. I just thought that there was one way to speak to my father and another to speak to my mother.

–Louis St. Laurent (1882–1973), prime minister

Sometimes I wish we had never described the official languages policy as "bilingualism"—because the word apparently implies that our intent is for all Canadians to learn two languages. Such is not our intent at all.

–Pierre Elliott Trudeau (1919–2000), prime minister

Can we not believe that in that supreme battle here, on the Plains of Abraham, when the fate of arms turned against us, can we not believe that it entered into the decrees of Providence that the two races, up to that time enemies, should henceforth live in peace and harmony, and henceforth should form one nation? Such was the inspired cause of Confederation.

–Sir Wilfrid Laurier (1841–1919), prime minister,
in an address in Québec City, June 24, 1889

There are two miracles in Canadian history. The first is the survival of French Canada, and the second is the survival of Canada.

–F.R. Scott (1899–1985), lawyer and poet,
by Ramsay Cook in *Canada and the French-Canadian Question* (1966)

Biculture? What breed of bull is that? I've heard of agriculture and horticulture, even floriculture and aviculture. But biculture?

–Eugene Whelan (1924–), MP, when he was discussing the
Royal Commission on Bilingualism and Biculturalism in 1965

Why can't we realize that since French Canada is not going to vanish, even if Québec becomes independent, we might just as well try to understand it. We might even enjoy it.

–Ramsay Cook (1931–), historian

To be honestly a Canadian, I shouldn't have to feel like a Native leaving his reservation every time I leave Québec. Outside Québec, I don't find two great cultures. I feel like a foreigner. First and foremost, I am a Québecois, and second—with a rather growing sense of doubt—a Canadian.

–René Lévesque (1922–87), Québec premier, in 1963

GREAT CONSTITUTIONAL DEBATES

If the country is going to be torn apart because we bring back from Britain our own constitution after 115 years of Confederation and after more than 50 years of fruitless discussions, and because we have asked for a Canadian charter of rights, when most of you already have provincial charters, then the country deserves to be torn up.

–Pierre Elliott Trudeau (1919–2000), prime minister

If we have been able to repatriate our Constitution from Britain, perhaps it's time to ask ourselves: should we repatriate our culture?

–Marcel Masse (1936–), MP, in 1985 when he was federal Minister of Communications

Where the hell is Meech Lake, anyway? Wherever the damn place is it's full of sleazy bastards up to no damn good.

–A comment heard uttered by a passing pedestrian in St. John's, Newfoundland in April 1990

As some people have been saying lately, "It's 'meech ado' about nothing."

–Barbara Frum (1937–92), broadcaster

Today has been a good day for Canada. Today's discussions have been marked by generosity and flexibility and, above all, the political will to find agreement in the spirit of compromise that characterizes the Canadian people.

–Brian Mulroney (1939–), prime minister, a sentiment he shared in 1987 after reaching an agreement with the provincial premiers on the unsuccessful Meech Lake Accord

TRUE, BLUE TORIES

The Tories enjoyed a strong showing in the House of Commons from 1984 to 1993, only to have their popularity crumble in 1993. Only two of the party's candidates survived the storm. Since then, the Conservative Party has rebuilt its ranks; re-examined its purpose, goals and visions; and was elected to a minority government in 2006.

Anyone who can bring the Conservative Party together can bring the country together.

–Joe Clark (1939–), prime minister,
when serving as Conservative leader in 1976

When that time comes, time has come for a change; but in the very nature of things a Conservative does not believe in change for the sake of change, nor does he believe that it is essential to make a change merely because you may alter a name. I think most of us believe with Tennyson: That man's the true Conservative/Who lops the moulder'd branch away.

–R.B. Bennett (1870–1947), prime minister

We have to build up a big blue machine that will steamroll over the Liberals and socialists in this province.

–George Drew (1894–1973),
Ontario premier, in 1948

You're considered to have a rare kind of social disease if you espouse neo-conservative ideas in Canada.

–Barbara Amiel (1940–), columnist

The day Canada's Conservative party changed its name to the Progressive Conservative party, it publicly acknowledged its philosophical weakness and its willingness to play prostitution politics. With that one stroke, it could abandon any true conservative vision of the world and do battle solely on the basis of out-promising the Liberals; two political parties hugging the centre to death from different sides.

–William D. Gairdner, academic and writer, in 1990

THE LIBERALS' FLAMING RED

Although in 1878 the Liberals boasted they were the "party of purity," they've had to weather a number of storms of their own.

When I was going to run I went to a thinkers' conference to find out if I really was a Liberal. I enjoyed it and got at what the party is. Same thing as being Presbyterian.

–Judy LaMarsh (1924–80), Liberal cabinet minister, in 1975

Individual members of the Liberal party may have done what they should not have done, but the whole party is not thereby disgraced. The party is not disgraced, but it is in the valley of humiliation.

–William Lyon Mackenzie King (1874–1950), prime minister, in 1931 after the Beauharnois Power inquiry.

An organized hypocrisy dedicated to getting and holding office.

–John W. Dafoe (1866–1944), journalist and liberal reformer, in 1919

The Liberals talk about a stable government, but we don't know how bad the stable is going to smell.

–Tommy Douglas (1904–86), leader of the NDP; Saskatchewan CCF premier

The Liberals in Saskatchewan are in Opposition, in Manitoba in hiding, in BC they're invisible and in Alberta they're a protected species.

–David Steuart, Saskatchewan Liberal leader, in 1975

I do not say that all Grits are horse thieves, but I feel quite sure that all horse thieves are Grits.

–Sir John A. Macdonald (1815–91), prime minister

We are in the extreme centre, the radical middle. That is our position.

–Pierre Elliott Trudeau (1919–2000), prime minister

A Liberal is a Liberal is a Liberal, except in opposition when he sounds like a New Democrat.

–Ed Broadbent (1936–), leader of the federal NDP

SPEAKING OF THE NDP

The NDP might be small, but they won't be ignored.

Give us 70 seats and we'll turn Parliament upside down. Give us 170 seats and we'll turn the country right side up.

–Tommy Douglas (1904–86), leader of the NDP; Saskatchewan CCF premier

Winning the leadership of the NDP, unless the party holds the balance of power in Parliament, is like coming first in the Florida Grapefruit League. Out there in the real world it doesn't count.

–Mordecai Richler (1931–2001), writer and cultural commentator

I often think that when people get into the polling booth, and they're just about to vote for us, the dead hand of their ghostly Liberal or Conservative grandfathers comes down and takes them.

–David Lewis (1909–81), politician

FREE TRADE... WELL, SOMETIMES

I invite the most ardent free trader in public life to present a plausible solution of this problem, and I contend that he is bound to do so before he talks of free trade as practicable in Canada...The thing is removed from the domain of practical politics.

–Edward Blake (1833–1912), lawyer and politician, in 1887

I must say that on principle I am a very strong freetrader. I have been fed and educated on free trade doctrines, but doctrines do not always apply to facts.

–Clifford Sifton (1861–1929), politician

Canada, having once become the commercial and industrial vassal of the United States, would inevitably become the political vassal of that country and ultimately be absorbed.

–Sir Robert Borden (1854–1937), prime minister, in 1911 when campaigning successfully against freer trade with the U.S.

You can help screw Ontario. Support free trade.

–Mordecai Richler (1931–2001), writer and cultural commentator

It's a bitter commentary on our 20th-century society that the very phrase "free trade" has come to have a hopelessly old-fashioned and unrealistic ring to it.

–Lester B. Pearson (1897–1972), prime minister, in 1957

We will not only be harmonized, we will be homogenized, and we will be hosed.

–John Turner (1929–), prime minister, giving his views on free trade in 1988

When I was going down to New York to make my name in this dismal business, my mother took me aside—even though I was a grown man—and said, "Leonard, you be careful. Those people aren't like we are." And that's all I have to say about the free-trade issue.

–Leonard Cohen (1934–), poet, author and singer, in 1988

This country could not survive with a policy of unfettered free trade. I'm all in favour of eliminating unfair protectionism, where it exists. This is a separate country. We'd be swamped. We have in many ways a branch-plant economy in certain important sectors. All that would happen with that kind of concept would be the boys cranking up their plants throughout the United States in bad times and shutting their entire branch plants in Canada. It's bad enough as it is.

–Brian Mulroney (1939–), prime minister, in 1983

Whatever little is left fluttering in the aftermath of this election, one thing is sure: the legacy of the trade debate will be a deeply divided country—the very thing Brian Mulroney once promised to repair.

–Margaret Atwood, writer, commenting on the 1988 election campaign

SOMETHING TO THINK ABOUT

"Everything happens for a reason." "If it doesn't rain, it pours." "Eat it up, wear it out, make it do, do without."…We've heard them all and many more…the maxims recited by rote by moms and dads and grandparents and others and received as the sage advice of our elders. We've been raised by them and most likely we're passing at least some on to our youngsters. Whether or not we agree with the sentiment, chances are we do stop and ponder them…if only for a moment or two.

TAKING THINGS PHILOSOPHICALLY

Taking things philosophically is easy if they don't concern you.

–"Eye-Opener Bob" Edwards (1864–1922), pioneer journalist

Everybody is trapped, more or less. The best thing you can hope for is to understand your trap and make terms with it, tooth by tooth.

–Robertson Davies (1913–95), writer

We are punished not for our sins but for our stupidity.

–Irving Layton (1912–2006), poet

If you're not annoying somebody, you're not really alive.

–Margaret Atwood (1939–), writer

The difference between people and rats is that people will keep heading down the same old tunnel even though the cheese is no longer there.

–Pamela Peck, Ph.D.,
cultural anthropologist and author of *The Cannibal's Cookbook*

It is never a sound policy to harbour a grudge or even to resent an injury, except when inspired by sheer malice.

–Sir Wilfrid Laurier (1841–1919), prime minister

WORDS OF WISDOM

If you wish to tell the truth, make people laugh. But if you wish to make people laugh, tell the truth.

–Camillien Houde (1889–1958), Montréal mayor

Really, sex and laughter do go very well together and I wondered—and I still do—which is more important.

–Hermione Gingold (1897–1987), actress

Diaper backward spells repaid. Think about it.

–Marshall McLuhan (1911–80), educator and media philosopher

Don't trouble trouble unless trouble troubles you.

–Guy Hudon, Dean of Law at Laval University, in 1980

He who studies medicine without books sails an uncharted sea, but he who studies medicine without patients does not go to sea at all.

–William Osler (1849–1919), physician

In Canadian culture, a liberated woman who wants a new life goes to the North and makes it with a bear. There must be a lesson in that somewhere, and I don't think it's good news for Canadian men.

–Martain Knelman, writer, in 1976

Fate, I thought. Who is equal to it? For to be equal to fate is to be equal to the knowledge that everything we have done, achieved, endured and been proud and ashamed of is nothing.

–Hugh MacLennan (1907–90), writer

Time solves every problem and in the process adds a couple of new ones.

–Richard J. Needham (1912–96), humour columnist

Avoid people who say: "Do you have a minute?" They take up the most time of all.

–Allan Fotheringham (1932–), media personality

As Robert Fulford once told me, if print had been invented after radio and television, it would be regarded as a wildly innovative medium—compact, portable, requiring only a brain for use.

–David Suzuki (1936–),
environmentalist, scientist and media personality

Persons are apt to deceive themselves as well as to be deceived, and having once fixed their minds on any one subject, will only read and believe those things that accord with their wishes.

–Catharine Parr Traill (1802–99), Ontario pioneer and writer

Everything has its astonishing, wondrous aspect, if you bring a mind to it that's really your own—a mind that hasn't been smeared and blurred with half-understood muck from schools, or the daily papers, or any other ragbag of reach-me-down notions.

–Robertson Davies (1913–95), writer

If a lady treads on a banana skin and sprinkles herself all over the sidewalk, a man will gallantly gather up the pieces and help her to place herself together again. But if his own wife meets with a similar misfortune, he gives her a piece of his mind.

–Kit Coleman (1864–1915), pioneer journalist

Here I would assert the ancient and forgotten doctrine that evil is, not the opposite, but the absence of good.

–George P. Grant (1918–88), philosopher

To me, morality is how you treat others.

–Gregory Baum (1923–), theologian

I don't see any point in making anything but controversial statements. There is no other way of getting any attention at all.

–Marshall McLuhan (1911–80), educator and media philosopher

Most forward-looking people have their heads turned sideways.

–Harold Adams Innis (1894–1952), historian

Leadership is the art of influencing others to do willingly what is required in order to achieve an aim or goal.

–Jacques A. Dextraze (1919–93),
Canadian soldier and Chief of the Defence Staff

One topic more and I have done. Society contains not the whole of man. Human societies die; man never dies. Man has a higher destiny than that of states.

–Egerton Ryerson (1803–82), educator

True wisdom is only to be found far away from people, out in the great solitude, and it is not found in play but only through suffering. Solitude and suffering open the human mind, and therefore a shaman must seek his wisdom there.

–Igjugarjuk, Inuit shaman, in 1930

LOOKING TO A HIGHER POWER

It's been said, "Nature is the glass reflecting God; those who are closest to it know the true meaning of love and peace." For a mystic like Emily Carr, God is experienced through everything in the natural world. For others, it's experienced more traditionally through the church proper. Still others look for spiritual guidance in the Eastern traditions. Faith and worship—along with critical reviews of such—are as unique as each individual.

The only thing worth striving for is to express God. Every living thing is God made manifest. All real art is the eternal seeking to express God, the one substance out of which all things are made. Search for the reality of each object, that is, its real and only beauty; recognize our relationship with all life; say to every animate and inanimate thing "brother"; be at one with all things, finding the divine in all; when one can do this, maybe one can paint.

–Emily Carr (1871–1945), artist and writer

We are asked why we prefer to be vagabonds rather than cloistered nuns, since the cloisters offer protection to persons of our sex. We reply that the Blessed Virgin was never cloistered but she never refused a voyage which allowed her to carry out some good or charitable deed. Because we see her as our teacher, we are not cloistered, although we live in a Community. In this way, we can go everywhere we are sent to educate girls.

–Marguerite Bourgeoys (1620–1700),
creator of Canada's first religious community responsible
for travelling through the wilderness and teaching children

Trust in God and She will provide.

–Charlotte Whitton (1896–1975), mayor of Ottawa

To attain in art is to rise above the external and temporary to the real of the eternal reality, to express the "I am," or God, in all life, in all growth, for there is nothing but God.

–Emily Carr (1871–1945), artist and writer

As a Buddhist I have always believed that we will all come together one day…and life would come full circle, bringing everything into a harmony.

–Asayo Murakami (1898–2002), Japanese immigrant

God in all. Always looking for the face of God, always listening for the voice of God in Nature. Nature is God revealing himself, expressing his wonders and his love, Nature clothed in God's beauty of holiness.

–Emily Carr (1871–1945), artist and writer

The story of the Jesuit missionaries to Canada is not only a great act in the national drama…it is a saga of the human race.

–E.J. Pratt (1882–1964), poet

The French won't take over and neither will the Pope, although he's not the menace he used to be.

–Pierre Elliott Trudeau (1919–2000), prime minister

I took a day to search for God
And found Him not. But as I trod
By rocky ledge, through woods untamed
Just where one scarlet lily flamed
I saw his footprint in the sod.

–Bliss Carman (1861–1929), poet

I can say that I do not think of God as a concept, but as an immediate and ever-present fact—an occasion for continuous dialogue.

–Marshall McLuhan (1911–80), educator and media philosopher

I do not believe in some kind of a Creator. I believe in the Holy Spirit. I think there is an informing spirit in the whole of creation but I also believe we have some kind of free will.

–Margaret Laurence (1926–87), writer

The misfortun' is, we are all apt to think Scriptur' intended for our neighbours, and not for ourselves.

–T.C. Haliburton (1796–1865), writer

Going to church doesn't make you a Christian any more than going to a garage makes you a car.

–Laurence J. Peter (1919–90), educator

I know it is hard to be hungry and be a Christian.

–Morley Callaghan (1903–90), writer

God punishes us mildly by ignoring our prayers and severely by answering them.

–Richard J. Needham (1912–96), columnist

The very energy of asking for help from Christ, God, Allah, the angels, is a catalyst for change and is as strong as the strength of my belief.

–Dorothy Maclean, medium, in 1980

It is the nature of most men to crave a spiritual lightning rod, a protection against the caprice of accident, the convulsions of nature, and the evil in other men's hearts.

–Mary Maxwell (1910–2000),
leading member of the Bahai Faith in Canada

Why must people kneel down to pray? If I really wanted to pray I'll tell you what I'd do. I'd go out into a great big field all alone or into the deep, deep woods, and I'd look up into the sky-up-up-up-into that lovely blue sky that looks as if there was no end to its blueness. And then I'd just feel a prayer.

–Lucy Maud Montgomery (1874–1942), writer

Religion is the drive toward transcendence, the thrust of man out of and beyond himself, out of and beyond the limited order under which he lives, in an attempt to open himself to the totality of existence and reach unlimited reality and ultimate value.

–Charles Davis, theologian, in 1974

WE GOT GAME

Canadians can boast some of the best athletes in the world.
We all know we created the best game of all time—hockey.
We hold our own in the big leagues.
And despite what Harold Ballard may have thought,
Canadian women know a thing or two about sport.

THE BATTLE IS NOT WITH THE MOUNTAIN

Climbers don't conquer mountains. The battle is not with the mountain but with themselves. The conquest occurs within the climber's mind in penetrating those self-imposed limitations and fears and getting through to that good stuff, that stuff called potential—most of which we rarely use—and it is only in that rare state of total commitment we begin to scrape the surface.

–Sharon Wood (1957–), mountaineer

Athletic maids to arms!...We are taking up the sword, and high time it is in defence of our so-called athletic bodies to give the lie to those pen flourishers who depict us not as paragons of feminine physique, beauty and health, but rather as Amazons and ugly ducklings all because we have become sports-minded.

–Fanny (Bobbie) Rosenfeld (1903–69),
named Canadian woman athlete of the half-century in 1949

You do not know who you really are until you know what you can fully achieve. That is what makes living worthwhile. You had to be the best, period.

–Sharon Wood (1957–), mountaineer

HOCKEY

I got into hockey because I wanted to be recognized in the streets.

–Peter Pocklington (1921–), owner of the Edmonton Oilers

FRUM: Listen, I just go for the hearts and flowers, so I'm there Saturday night…
BALLARD: They shouldn't let females on the radio anyway. They're a joke…You know where they're good…You know where they're good, doncha?…You know where they're at their best, doncha?…

–From a controversial radio interview between host Barbara Frum and Harold Ballard, owner of the Toronto Maple Leafs, March 5, 1979

How would you like a job where, every time you make a mistake, a big red light goes on and 18,000 people boo?

–Attributed to hockey player Jacques Plante in 1985

All pro athletes are bilingual. They speak English and profanity.

–Gordie Howe (1928–), hockey player and commentator

During one game I was shouting, "He shoots! He scores!" when my voice suddenly soared to a note so high that even a Metropolitan Opera soprano would have envied me. Quickly I apologetically remarked, "I almost blew a fuse on that one." Soon there arrived from widely scattered sources every type of fuse that man had devised.

–Foster Hewitt (1902–85), hockey broadcaster

Every boy in Canada who owns a pair of skates hopes to play for Toronto when he grows up—and most of the good ones do!

–Conn Smythe (1895–1980), hockey personality

Dreams really do come true, I thought to myself as I sat in the stands of Maple Leaf Gardens on that September day in 1973 when I first reported to the Toronto Maple Leafs. The building was dark, and I wanted to be alone, just to have time to think…I'd finally made it. There I was at the Gardens, about to begin playing for the Maple Leafs, the team I had cheered for like crazy as a kid.

–Lanny McDonald (1953–), hockey player

If you can't beat 'em in the alley, you can beat 'em on the ice.

–Conn Smythe (1895–1980), hockey personality

Who wants to be Prime Minister if he can be Maple Leaf captain?

–Dick Beddoes (1926–91), hockey personality, in 1989

There's a difference between a hockey player and a football player or a baseball player. It's that hockey guys play if they can breathe.

–Conn Smythe (1895–1980), hockey personality

When I want your opinion, I'll give it to you.

–Harold Ballard (1903–90), owner of the Toronto Maple Leafs

INTERVIEWER: You can't spell "goal," much less score one.
SHACK (After scoring a goal, spelling loudly): S-C-O-R-E.

–Exchange between Maple Leafs right wing Eddie Shack and an unidentified sports reporter in the 1960s

Hockey has always been Canada's game. We still play it better than anyone else in the world, and I wish I could lace up my skates right now, and get out there and help keep it that way!

–Fred "Cyclone" Taylor (1885–1979), hockey star

Gretzky is something else again...He strikes me as the first nondescript hockey star. Sometimes you don't even realize he's out there, watching as he whirls, until he emerges out of nowhere, finding open ice, and accelerating to a score... Watching him out there, I've often felt he's made of Plasticine...Gretzky is arguably the best player hockey has ever known.

–Mordecai Richler (1931–2001), writer

Baseball can have its perfect dimensions, its undeniable drama, but hockey, for all its wrongs, still has the potential to deliver a momentary, flashing magic that is found in no other game we play.

–Roy MacGregor (1948–), columnist, in 1987

ABOUT THE AUTHOR

Lisa Wojna, author of two other non-fiction books, has worked in the community newspaper industry as a writer and journalist and has travelled all over Canada, from the windy prairies of Manitoba to northern British Columbia, and even to the wilds of Africa. Although writing and photography have been a central part of her life for as long as she can remember, it's the people behind every story that are her motivation and give her the most fulfilment.